Institutional Assessment for Self-Improvement

Richard I. Miller
Guest Editor

Jossey-Bass Inc., Publishers
San Francisco • Washington • London

LB
2331.63
.I57

INSTITUTIONAL ASSESSMENT FOR SELF-IMPROVEMENT
New Directions for Institutional Research
Volume VIII, Number 1, 1981
　　　Richard I. Miller, Guest Editor

Copyright © 1981 by Jossey-Bass Inc., Publishers
　　　　　　　　　and
　　　　　　　Jossey-Bass Limited

Copyright under International, Pan American, and Universal
Copyright Conventions. All rights reserved. No part of
this issue may be reproduced in any form—except for brief
quotation (not to exceed 500 words) in a review or professional
work—without permission in writing from the publishers.

New Directions for Institutional Research (publication number
USPS 098-830) is published quarterly by Jossey-Bass Inc., Publishers,
and is sponsored by the Association for Institutional Research.
Subscriptions are available at the regular rate for institutions,
libraries, and agencies of $30 for one year. Individuals may
subscribe at the special professional rate of $18 for one year.
New Directions is numbered sequentially—please order extra
copies by sequential number. The volume and issue numbers
above are included for the convenience of libraries.

Correspondence:
Subscriptions, single-issue orders, change of address notices,
undelivered copies, and other correspondence should be sent to
New Directions Subscriptions, Jossey-Bass Inc., Publishers,
433 California Street, San Francisco, California 94104.

Editorial correspondence should be sent to the Editor-in-Chief,
Marvin W. Peterson, Center for the Study of Higher Education,
University of Michigan, Ann Arbor, Michigan 48109.

Library of Congress Catalogue Card Number LC 80-84288
International Standard Serial Number ISSN 0271-0579
International Standard Book Number ISBN 87589-841-6

Cover design by Willi Baum
Manufactured in the United States of America

Contents

Editor's Notes   Richard I. Miller   **vii**

Reputational Ratings and   Judith K. Lawrence   **1**
Undergraduate Education Assessment   Lewis C. Solmon

    The authors present the preliminary findings from a pilot study which uses the reputational rating approach to assess quality at the undergraduate level.

Some Theoretical and Practical   H. R. Kells   **15**
Suggestions for Institutional Assessment

    Recent studies and experience indicate that useful assessment processes can be designed and managed effectively and that "assessment for what?" is a critical question.

Strategies for Assessing   Donald Tritschler   **27**
Performance at Your Own
Institution

    Experiments at fifteen New York colleges demonstrate how to establish continuous, objective self-assessment systems which, by addressing a school's own concerns, go beyond the purposes of accreditation.

Relationships Between Regional   William E. Troutt   **45**
Accrediting Association Standards
and Educational Quality

    Comparing regional accreditation standards to research on student achievement suggests that any indirect approach to assessing institutional performance rests on a frail empirical basis.

European Perspectives Suggest   John Sizer   **61**
Other Criteria

    The nature of institutional performance is changing under conditions of financial stringency, possible contraction, and changing needs.

Some Concluding Remarks   Richard I. Miller   **89**

    The preceding chapters developed many valuable tools for institutional self-assessment, but the critical point is that evaluation must be a means and not an end.

Index   **93**

The Association for Institutional Research was created in 1966 to benefit, assist, and advance research leading to improved understanding, planning, and operation of institutions of higher education. Publication policy is set by its Publications Board.

PUBLICATIONS BOARD
Gerald W. McLaughlin (Chairperson), Virginia Polytechnic Institute and State University
Alfred A. Cooke, Institute for Service to Education, Washington, D.C.
John A. Lucas, William Rainey Harper College, Palatine, Illinois
Marilyn McCoy, National Center for Higher Education Management Systems, Boulder, Colorado
Marvin W. Peterson, University of Michigan
Joan S. Stark, University of Michigan

EX-OFFICIO MEMBERS OF THE PUBLICATIONS BOARD
Mary E. Corcoran, University of Minnesota
Charles Elton, University of Kentucky
Douglas Mathewson, University of Nevada
Richard R. Perry, University of Toledo

EDITORIAL ADVISORY BOARD
All members of the Publications Board and:
Frederick E. Balderston, University of California, Berkeley
Howard R. Bowen, Claremont Graduate School
Roberta D. Brown, Arkansas College
Robert M. Clark, University of British Columbia
Lyman A. Glenny, University of California, Berkeley
David S. P. Hopkins, Stanford University
Roger G. Schroeder, University of Minnesota
Robert J. Silverman, Ohio State University
Martin A. Trow, University of California, Berkeley

Editor's Notes

Institutional appraisal will be used more and more during the 1980s. In one respect it is the logical next step of the groundswell of faculty evaluation that started around 1972 and of administrative evaluation which followed a few years later.

Institutional evaluation goes back to the earliest days of higher education and one can imagine that a robust evaluative dialogue must have taken place in Ancient Greece between the merits of Isocrates and his school for orators and Aristotle and his academy. Current institutional evaluation can be traced to the rise of the accrediting associations at the turn of the century. There is some nostalgia for the simpler approach that was outlined by President Richard H. Jesse of the University of Missouri in his address at the first meeting of the North Central Association in 1896. In naming the essential characteristics of a college, he said: "A college must have . . at least eight good instructors who devote their whole time to teaching in the freshman or higher classes" (Zook and Haggerty, 1936).

With the complexities of organizational structures in 1980, creative frugality the watchword for resource use, greater demands from state legislators for institutional justification, fiscal pressures combining with shrinking enrollment to diminish morale, and tendencies toward organizational disintegration within no-growth institutions, it is imperative that educational professionals take the initiative in developing sound, practical approaches to institutional evaluation. This volume is directed toward this objective.

In Chapter One, Judith K. Lawrence and Lewis C. Solmon present some preliminary findings from a pilot study which assesses quality at the undergraduate level using the reputational rating approach in seven fields: biology, business, chemistry, economics, English, history, and sociology. In reviewing the literature, the authors find that ratings, literally, are due to the nature of the evaluation techniques. They contend that while it is increasingly popular to allege that evaluation must be referenced to individual program goals, it has yet to be demonstrated that quantification of subjective opinions is inferior to quantifications of so-called indicators when national assessments are conducted.

In the second chapter, H. R. Kells writes about the realities of institutional assessment and concludes the prospect is not encouraging.

He contends, "The overall picture is frantic, troubled, and difficult to comprehend; and neither campus leaders nor other professionals have a clear sense of how to go about their task. They do not seem to bring the same level of professionalism to tasks like assessment or planning that they surely must apply in the pursuit of knowledge in their own discipline."

Donald Tritschler, in Chapter Three, develops some findings and conclusions from a FIPSE-sponsored project in which fifteen private and public postsecondary institutions in New York State developed self-assessment programs on their respective campuses. Tritschler found that the common difficulty for individuals and organizations is in being objective about themselves. Additionally, there is no dependable way to sustain an effort that is added onto what faculty and staff already do. The process is impossible without active faculty participation but their known priorities are teaching and research. Faculty are isolated from each other and often feel they cannot act appropriately on matters outside their expertise. The chief executive officer must establish the value of this activity for the entire institution.

In Chapter Four, William E. Troutt states that to be useful in determining correlation of education quality, research must satisfy the following criteria: employ measures of intellectual achievement or cognitive outcomes, collect data from contrasting types of institutions, and provide information on student change between admission and a specified later time. Troutt found only four institutional studies that survived this screening process.

He determined that the five quality assurance standards for regional accrediting associations are: the institution's purposes and objectives, educational program, financial resources, faculty, and library/learning center. His review of available research could not substantiate the claim that certain accrediting associations standards assure institutional quality. This review also illustrated the difficulty in authoritatively stating that research demonstrates the lack of any relationship between accrediting standards and institutional quality.

John Sizer, in the fifth chapter, gives a European perspective. He believes that six standards—relevance, verifiability, freedom from bias, quantifiability, economic feasibility, and institutional acceptability—can be applied to existing and proposed performance indicators. He argues that during uncertain times, "high-quality managers of change of appropriate academic standing" should be motivating their institutions to become effective in the long term. This can be done by examining the future environment, communicating implications for the future to institutional constituencies, developing priorities for evaluating the current program, and setting the future goals and objectives of the institution.

Richard I. Miller has written a short concluding chapter. The references and citations used by the respective authors constitute an extensive and current bibliography. For additional bibliographical references, please see Lawrence and Green (1980) and Miller (1979).

A word of special appreciation to each of the authors is in order. All are busy people yet they saw the general topic to be of sufficient importance to warrant their attention. The high quality of their contributions will provide additional thought in the very important area of institutional evaluation.

Richard I. Miller
Guest Editor

References

Lawrence, J. K., and Green, K. C. *A Question of Quality: The Higher Education Ratings Game.* AAHE-ERIC Higher Education Research Report No. 5. Washington, D.C.: American Association for Higher Education, 1980.

Miller, R. I. *The Assessment of College Performance.* San Francisco: Jossey-Bass, 1979.

Zook, G. F., and Haggerty, M. E. *The Evaluation of Higher Institutions.* Chicago: University of Chicago Press, 1936.

Richard I. Miller is visiting fellow in the Department of Education at Cornell University. He is author of three Jossey-Bass books on evaluation, the most recent being The Assessment of College Performance *(1979).*

A pilot study of undergraduate institutions tests the value of the reputational rating approach. This approach, which uses subjective questionnaires, may be both effective and economically feasible.

Reputational Ratings and Undergraduate Education Assessment

Judith K. Lawrence
Lewis C. Solmon

The higher education system in the United States represents the major forum for the advancement of human knowledge, yet there is some irony in the fact that the system cannot effectively assess its own performance. This chapter explores the reputational rating approach to evaluating the nation's colleges and universities. The chapter overviews past studies and describes a pilot study of undergraduate quality conducted by the Higher Education Research Institute (HERI) which uses this approach.

This approach has generated a number of concerns related to concept and method that provide a basis for considering issues fundamental to performance assessment of colleges and universities, especially at the undergraduate level. Even as the system enters a decade

The study described in this chapter is supported by a grant from the Exxon Education Foundation.

when this capacity would seem to be imperative, each attempt is met with very real criticisms; each resolution of specific criticisms is met with further legitimate criticisms; and the quandary increases. In this respect, the preliminary findings of the HERI pilot study may lead some to advocate abandonment of the reputational rating approach. However, the study also raises important considerations in performance assessments in higher education. The existence of subjective judgments is implicit in evaluations, and the extent of their role in higher education must not be underestimated.

Especially in the early half of this century, the views of eminent alumni were pervasive in assessing the performance of the nation's colleges and universities. However, this approach ignored the fact that certain institutions attracted people destined to have productive careers— regardless of the extent to which they would benefit from college. Since then, the key studies conducted to differentiate the top domain have been reputational ratings of graduate departments. These include the pioneering studies of Hughes (1925, 1934); the rating of graduate departments derived through a self-study of the University of Pennsylvania (Keniston, 1959); and those sponsored by the American Council on Education (ACE) during the days of deliberate diversification and expansion in U.S. higher education (Cartter, 1966; Roose and Andersen, 1970).

Reputational rating studies of the U.S. higher education system have employed rather consistent methodologies over time and across domains such as graduate education, professional education, and the undergraduate level. Hughes set the precedents, but Cartter refined— if not defined—the approach.

The common components of reputational rating studies are as follows. The departmental specialization is the unit of analysis, rather than the institution. Raters are faculty members of a field and are asked either to rate departments from a list of institutions on a scale (recognition method) or to list five or more outstanding departments in their respective fields (recall method). The rating criterion is generally agreed to be faculty eminence through scholarship; when employed in conjunction with a measure concerning preparation of doctoral students, the correlation is generally .9 (Cartter, 1966). Thus faculty are conceived as experts, and reputational ratings represent a kind of systemwide peer review of the top domain of higher education.

Reputational studies have been conducted across most fields and levels of U.S. higher education. Especially at the graduate level, the results have been rather consistent from study to study. It has been popular to aggregate departmental ratings into overall institutional ratings (Magoun 1966; Morgan, Kearney, and Regens, 1976); and reputations have frequently been shown to correlate with quantifiable indicators of both human and material resources in higher education, from sheer institutional size to library holdings to financial resources to alumni achievements.

In effect, the consistent results of reputational ratings of graduate programs have confirmed the folklore: Some institutions are more prestigious and more highly regarded within academe than are others. And in part, this is literally due to the nature of the evaluation techniques.

Whether overtly stated or not, visibility in higher education (hence reputation) rests on the eminence of faculty — especially at the graduate level. Faculty achieve eminence through publication, and peer review of publication underpins the academic reward system. The import of publication has increased in this century and remains the most substantial means for the academic community to evidence and evaluate the advancement of human knowledge. However, under the constant expansion and diversification of higher education, research publication and its attending visibility have come to be concentrated, protected, prioritized, and perpetuated in a handful of colleges and universities. Thus the nature of the inquiry, peer review of faculty excellence, inexorably leads to lists of those institutions (which are generally the same over time) that attract and employ productive, research-oriented faculty.

In identifying the top domain of graduate level colleges and universities, researchers have contended that the overall purpose of reputational ratings has been to inform the higher education community about excellent departments. As the system has changed, however, researchers have expressed correspondingly complex rationales for conducting their studies. In other words, the basis for filling the information "need" through reputational rating studies has changed during the century.

As president of Miami University of Ohio in 1925 and of the University of Iowa in 1934, Hughes's studies were concurrent with the establishment of graduate education and proliferation of specializations. Hence his rationale for conducting his studies was a simple one: Undergraduates required some means to decide where to attend graduate school in various fields. Scholarship and the advancement of knowledge constituted the fundamental missions of graduate education, and assessment criteria quite logically focused on faculty eminence as judged by peers.

Graduate education received a major impetus following Sputnik. Thus Keniston's 1959 rating (part of a comparative self-study at the University of Pennsylvania) was timely in itself. However, Keniston harkened back to Hughes's studies and claimed (p. 116) that a comparison of his predecessor's results with his study informed the system of "what changes have taken place in the course of a generation."

It was the ACE studies in general, and Cartter in particular, that introduced and generated the greatest complexity and controversy in the reputational rating approach to identifying excellence in U.S. graduate education. The stated purposes of the Cartter study were threefold: to update the Hughes and Keniston studies; to establish a basis for decisions about impending expansion in higher education; and to address—if not remedy—methodological concerns (particularly with respect to comparing quantitive indicators with the reputational rating approach). Above all, Cartter asserted, "Diversity can be a costly luxury if it is accomplished by ignorance" (1966, p. 3).

Yet by the appearance of the ACE replicational update of the Cartter study five years later, Roose and Andersen (1970) purported to be merely filling Cartter's (p. 8) promise not to let institutional reputations be "writ in stone." More than 26,000 copies of the Cartter report had been distributed by 1970, and the authors could not caution the higher education community enough about what the update was not, and the uses to which it ought not be put. The ACE ratings had provoked tremendous controversy about comparative, competitive assessments of higher education.

In the 1980s, resources for higher education are scarce. Limited resources—both human and financial—provide a persuasive rationale for assessing performance of institutions of higher education on a national scale. And of utmost concern is the safeguarding of those programs that are especially excellent.

HERI Pilot Study

In many respects, the HERI study of the reputations of undergraduate departments parallels the ACE design. It was preceded by a massive literature review of quality assessment approaches (Lawrence and Green, 1980). An attempt was made to rectify a number of major limitations in previous reputational rating studies, particularly with respect to the scope of the undergraduate level and of rating criteria. Previous studies have provoked criticism for omitting departments of merit and for failing to probe or promote excellence in dimensions other than scholarly productivity. The present study also explores the feasibility of rating undergraduate departments in a controlled, consistent manner—in contrast to those of Gourman (1977) or to popular college guides. (See Lawrence and Green, 1980, for discussions of undergraduate ratings.) Thus the immediate intent of the HERI pilot study is to quantify the subjective judgments of undergraduate departmental quality on multiple dimensions. Subjective judgments do form the basis for substantial decision making in higher education, and not only in the top domain.

The study is also designed to investigate a number of other elements in assessing undergraduate quality through the reputational approach: the association of ratings on different criteria and for different types of institutions; how ratings relate to measures of human and material resources at the undergraduate level; and which (if any) of these ratings are associated with educational impact. Above all, the validity of such judgments—or the lack thereof—needs examination.

Other areas of inquiry in this pilot study concern the effects on undergraduate ratings of the type of rater, rating criteria, domain of the system assessed, and the unit of analysis. In the reputational rating approach, results may be inextricably tied to the precedents set in previous reputational studies.

Study Design. The Education Directory was employed to provide the names of approximately 15,000 respondents from four states for rating seven departmental specializations. Raters for each field are department members in respective fields at four-year colleges and universities in California, Illinois, North Carolina, and New York. Lists of faculty from the Education Directory have been widely used by researchers. They are subject to some errors in field attributions, but cost and time considerations, and their overall comprehensiveness, justified their use. Departmental specializations included in the study are biology, business, chemistry, economics, English, history, and sociology. Both the selections of states and of fields are meant to reflect the diverse range of American undergraduate systems and of academic specializations, as well as net migration patterns in the U.S. population.

Overall, the HERI study used two bases for developing lists of four-year institutions to be rated by field. Despite the strong identifications of institutions with their state higher education systems, it is clear that some colleges have national visibility in drawing from and serving all areas of the country. Many institutions may not have national visibility; rather, they attract and serve local or regional populations and their needs—and they fulfill a range of missions which have heretofore received inadequate attention in quality assessments in higher education. For the present study, then, two lists of institutions were developed in each discipline and state—a "national" list and a "state" list. The prevailing assumption in developing lists of institutions was that errors of omission were more critical than errors of commission.

Using data from the 1977 Higher Education General Information Survey (HEGIS), we included an institution on the state list if at least five baccalaureate degrees had been granted that year in the respective field. This minimum selection criterion was used to allow for maximum inclusion of the diverse range of undergraduate colleges in each of the four states.

Selection criteria for the lists of nationally known institutions were more complex, and an institution was listed if it met any one of six criteria. These criteria included college choice data from the Cooperative Institutional Research Program files, the most recent Gourman rating of undergraduate institutions (Gourman, 1977), and 1977 HEGIS data.

An alternative to the recognition method of presenting lists of institutions for respondents to rate is the recall method, whereby raters are asked to generate the names of colleges and universities themselves. Since a priority of the HERI study was to reflect the breadth, scope, and diversity of undergraduate quality, the survey instrument purposefully included large numbers of colleges and universities. Moreover, respondents were given the option to write in names of institutions which were of high merit even though they failed to meet the selection criteria—thus providing a small recall component.

Altogether, separate alphabetized lists of national and in-state institutions in each of the seven fields and four states (twenty-eight in all) were developed. For the obvious reason that a number of institutions in each state met criteria for inclusion either as a national institution or as a state institution, the actual compositions of lists were varied slightly, and thirty-two lists were actually generated. In five fields (biology, business, economics, English, and history) nationally selected institutions in each state were presented within the in-state lists. To examine possible effects stemming from how institutions were listed, sociology and chemistry lists in California and New York were varied. In California, sociology and chemistry lists placed nationally selected California institutions on the national list for half of respondents. In New York, half of respondents were presented with all sociology and chemistry departments—national and in-state—in alphabetical order.

The number of departments on the twenty-eight lists (or thirty-two versions) ranged from a low of 85 to a high of 181. It is to be expected that few respondents will be knowledgeable enough to be able to rate them all.

Using a five-point scale, respondents are asked to mark the number which corresponds to their assessments of undergraduate departments listed for six criteria. The terms in the scoring scale are modifications of those employed in the ACE-sponsored ratings of graduate programs (Cartter, 1966; Roose and Andersen, 1970). The continuum on which respondents are asked to rate undergraduate departments includes outstanding, superior, average, marginal, and poor, as well as "no information."

Respondents are asked to rate six attributes of quality of undergraduate departments at the institutions. Some attributes are included to replicate previous investigations of quality in the higher education system and, thus, to reexamine their import in undergraduate education compared to the graduate domain (where previous peer assessments of higher education quality have been most addressed). Others are offered for the first time in reflection of the unique nature of undergraduate education and to examine how closely associated are different aspects of perceived quality. Moreover, different criteria are appropriate to different specializations.

Scholarly and professional accomplishments of the faculty bring their departments to the attention of the greater academic community, and have traditionally been the basis of the academic reward system. This factor can also serve as a marker variable, enabling this undergraduate survey to compare its results with the many previous reputational ratings at the graduate level. In undergraduate education, however, the teaching function is perhaps more critical. Thus both dimensions of faculty quality are included in the questionnaire. Respondents are asked to evaluate departments at the institutions listed on the questionnaire for (1) the scholarly and professional accomplishments of the faculty, (2) faculty commitment to undergraduate teaching, and (3) the overall quality of undergraduate education in their fields.

In order to increase access to and educational opportunity within American higher education, the current system has expanded and diversified to accommodate students with wide ranges of background preparation, abilities, and aspirations. Therefore, the evaluation options regarding students at undergraduate departments ask respondents to consider the quality of (4) preparation of students for graduate or professional school, and (5) preparation of students for employment after college.

The pluralistic undergraduate system not only serves many functions and many different student populations, different types of institutions have been shown to influence or "lead" other institutions differently (Johnson, 1978). Thus, respondents are asked to rate undergraduate departments in their fields for (6) the innovativeness of their curriculum or pedagogy. Of concern under retrenchment, innovation in generating new ideas and approaches is also important to improve or enhance undergraduate education.

Reputational ratings have routinely been criticized for halo effects, and their results have been undermined on the basis of inadequacy of information possessed by raters regarding the massive higher education system. Thus the questionnaire asks for background information about raters and about their attitudes toward quality assessments. Background questions about raters concern gender, current primary position, where raters have previously taught in their disciplines, the institutions from which they have earned degrees, and the colleges and universities attended by their children.

The importance of ten activities for promotion and tenure at their current institutions is assessed in order to distinguish among diverse goals and objectives being faced by individual raters. Respondents are asked to mark either "very important," "somewhat important," or "not important" for each of eleven items. These include scholarly productivity; quality of classroom undergraduate teaching; quality of undergraduate advising and other student contact; national public service; community service; provision of expertise for pay through faculty consulting and part-time employment; professional activities outside the institution (such as speaking, conferences, professional association duties); administrative services to institution; success of graduates in being admitted to graduate or professional school; success of graduates in obtaining employment; and quality of graduate teaching. (Four of the six criteria on which respondents are asked to rate departments appear on this list.)

A recent study suggests that different respondent groups and rating criteria lead to different rating results (Clark, Hartnett, and Baird, 1976). Thus in another question, the HERI survey raters are asked to indicate how accurately various constituencies would be able to evaluate the quality of undergraduate departments in their fields. The constituency groups include senior administrators (presidents, deans), other administrators (registrars, admissions officers, student services staff), senior faculty, junior faculty, students currently enrolled, alumni, employers, parents, state government agencies, and accrediting associations or professional associations "in your field."

Concluding the questionnaire, the final item asks, "Assuming you had a child majoring in your field who could gain admission to and afford to attend any higher education institution in the country, which three undergraduate institutions would you like that child to attend?" Investigations of the college preferences of students have suggested that there is a kind of folklore among students regarding the better undergraduate institutions (Astin and Solmon, 1979). It will be interesting to compare student and faculty preferences, not to mention examining to which undergraduate institutions the faculty in American higher education would send their own children.

By design, the HERI pilot study is comparative: of fields of specialization, of geographic aras, of nationally prominent and regional four-year institutions, of criteria for rating the undergraduate system, and of results in light of methodological manipulations. The data are still being collected at this time.

Preliminary Findings. As previously noted, a prevailing concern in this pilot study is to extend the assessment of undergraduate quality beyond a top domain reputed for scholarly productivity. Accordingly, the questionnaires present large numbers of departments and multiple-rating criteria. The extent to which these components make this study more comprehensive in scope than are previous reputational rating studies, however, threatens to affect the response rate.

A number of potential respondents have written with a range of comments as to why they have not rated departments in their fields. Some find the time commitment burdensome, while others are overwhelmed by how inadequate is their knowledge about departments (other than where they are currently employed). Some are disconcerted by simultaneous juxtapositions of different types of institutions, their placements on a national or state list, and rating criteria. Still others wonder about specific omissions (other than our errors, which occurred in biology and business in some states). Such reactions were not unanticipated. However, they do suggest that side effects accompany remedies to limitations in earlier reputational rating studies.

Still there are those who have filled out and returned the questionnaires, many of whom have written to applaud this pilot study. Given the general interest in the results of graduate reputational ratings, and in anticipation of retrenchment decisions in the coming decade in higher education, they have claimed a sense of obligation to assist in a national effort to assess reputational quality at the undergraduate level. It is clear that subjective judgments do come into play with respect to undergraduate education. Where to attend college, whom to admit, resource allocations, staffing decisions, and so forth entail comparisons between programs and institutions. Within the natural tendency for subjective judgments to occur, multiple dimensions contribute to the continuum of excellence in U.S. higher education. By including a range of rating criteria and departments, the HERI pilot study taps into the deliberate diversity of undergraduate education and into the breadth of knowledge the higher education community possesses about it. Perhaps some raters were fearful of self-incrimination with respect to the diversity of undergraduate education, to their own subjective judgments, or to their own institutions.

Certainly, with between 85 and 181 departments listed on a questionnaire to rate on six dimensions, the instrument is time consuming. Had cutoff criteria in selecting institutions been more stringent, however, multiple dimensions served by undergraduate education would have been cut off, along with the opportunity to include so wide a range of departmental diversity for rating. Furthermore, it is inevitable that various departments will be rated accordingly low or accordingly high in the HERI pilot study. Hence, restrictive alternatives were intentionally traded off in favor of extending the scope of the study.

It is to be expected that surveys that request respondents to answer questions about themselves would yield higher response rates than the rating section of the HERI study—especially given the relative comprehensiveness of its approach. It is also expected that vast numbers of respondents will employ the "insufficient information" option for lots of institutions (regardless of rating criteria).

The irony is that most faculty would willingly advise new high school graduates about the colleges to which they should apply. Perhaps the specificity of the criteria is especially discomfiting, in combination with the breadth of a diverse undergraduate system. This may ultimately reflect the tension between egalitarianism and elitism that prevails—indeed, is institutionalized—in the undergraduate system.

With respect to the validity of broadened approaches to reputational rating studies, the underlying issue is how much is known by how many faculty about how many departments of undergraduate education. Clearly, the visibility of institutional or departmental performance varies considerably by criterion; different constituencies possess different information as regards each criterion, and the import of criteria of excellence varies by specialization. This study will examine questions of validity and these variations.

Critical Issues

Comparative, competitive assessments are consistent with the American spirit, as is the making of the distinction of ultimate superiority. Reputational ratings of college and university programs traditionally identify a top domain in terms of one criterion. As such, they reinforce a folklore that some programs or institutions are "better" than others and, indeed, that some are "best." But egalitarianism and pluralism are also consistent with the American spirit and antithetical to hierarchical distinctions. This tension underlies the standard reputational rating approach to assessing the performance of colleges and universities, and the HERI study attempts to accommodate it.

Indeed, both hierarchies and egalitarianism characterize the nation's higher education system. Their dual characteristics are evidenced in many dimensions: lack of centralized federal control; preference for state control of the public domain; existence of private as well as public institutions; leveling of degree structures by institutional type (community college, four-year college, university); faculty staffing patterns and reward structures (community college faculty do not necessarily hold doctorates and are rewarded for teaching, whereas university appointees hold doctorates and are rewarded for publishing); variance in the degree and type of selectivity in admissions; the cumulative sorting and screening that occurs in the hierarchical degree structure — and so on. This deliberate diversity serves both elitism and egalitarianism, but it wreaks havoc in comparative, competitive assessments of program or institutional performance when assessment criteria are limited to the priorities of one type of institution or program.

Top Domain. Reputational studies tend to identify between ten and twenty top institutions, whether they concern graduate, professional, or undergraduate programs. Considering both the size of the higher education system in the U.S. and its deliberate diversity (from institutional types to specializations to degree levels), a unidimensional identification of a top domain is a critical issue.

Even at the doctoral level, some 400 institutions grant the degree. However, the pre-1920 institutions have granted most of the PhDs over the past half-century (National Research Council, 1978). The focus on the top domain yields no constructive information to the others regarding means of improvement or even their unique strengths. And when rank orders are presented, institutions manifest great concern about their appearance in or absence from the pecking order.

Nevertheless, the identification of seats of excellence in higher education is worthwhile. Especially as regards the undergraduate level, the ability to yield useful performance assessments rests on avoiding exclusive reference to an elitist or hierarchical model. Rather, performance assessment should extend to the egalitarian dimensions of U.S. undergraduate education. This we have attempted to do in our pilot study. Future comparisons might be between similar types of programs. However, then protests would be raised by certain departments that disapprove of the group in which they are classified, and larger comparisons would require another kind of assessment—that of evaluating the relative import of diverse functions and goals in undergraduate education. But that is a different question than how well particular departments stack up on a given dimension.

Education. In a recent speech, Astin (1980) noted that academics frequently refer to their teaching loads, yet do not similarly refer to their research loads. If there is one consensual mission of higher education, it is surely the education of students. Furthermore, this nation's higher education system is not unique in the sorting and screening function it serves. Human and material resources are distributed on a hierarchy in undergraduate education (Astin, 1977) and the measurement of how they are used poses a major challenge. This difficulty, too, is part of the tension between elitist and egalitarian elements in the nation's undergraduate system.

The obvious illustration is the comparison between the person who scores over 800 on an SAT test and another who scores in the bottom percentile. Upon leaving college, the high-aptitude graduate—and the selective institution that admitted him or her on that basis—is credited with educational excellence. The low-aptitude graduate, having begun at the two-year college, transferred to a four-year public institution, and passed muster to graduate, however, may have learned more and may actually represent better institutional performance.

In themselves, human and material resources are merely "input" to programs and institutions. This must be kept in perspective in assessing the actual performance of colleges and universities. "Inputs" must not be considered synonymous with excellence when their quantifications are extremely high, nor be confused with the subsequent educational impact in higher education assessments.

Quality. In light of the diversity in U.S. higher education, quality (like beauty) may be in the eye of the beholder. Compared to what? constitutes a central issue in its identification as well. Does quality in higher education exist on a continuum? Or are there aspects of the system which are of absolute quality or excellence or superiority? Where is a continuum of quality appropriate, and where is such a continuum inadequate—if not intolerable?

The reputational rating approach has been employed, and challenged by other approaches, for over half a century in higher education quality assessments. It has yielded equivocal answers to questions like the above. Yet it has also helped to raise them and even to bring them into focus. Regardless of which component of the system is being assessed, it is clear that views on the meaning of quality depend upon whose opinions and values are being tapped.

Cartter (1966) pointed out that so-called objective indicators of quality in higher education (like library size or publications) are ultimately subjective criteria of quality only once removed. In performance assessments, it is important to understand the subjective nature in identifications of attributes of quality—even before they are quantified.

Summary and Conclusions

There is no dearth of critics of the reputational rating approach in studies of quality in U.S. higher education. Nonetheless, subjective judgments do form the basis for substantial decision making in the system. A pilot study of undergraduate reputations in seven fields in four states (still in the field) promises valuable information about this evaluation technique when broader assessment criteria and institutional diversity are incorporated. A preliminary finding is that such broadening generates massive survey instruments, and in turn may reduce response rates. In this respect, like many drug treatments for illness, side effects show up that must be weighed against the original symptoms.

It is increasingly popular to allege that evaluation in higher education must be referenced to individual program goals. But it has yet to be demonstrated that quantification of subjective opinions is inferior to quantifications of so-called objective indicators when national assessments are conducted. In a cost-benefit sense, in-depth site visits and interviews with students, alumni, and employers, as well as faculty, would be impossibly expensive on so large a scale. And under retrenchment, comparisons must be made in broad, consistent terms.

The challenge in performance assessment—and the HERI pilot study promises to contribute to meeting it—is for the nation's higher education system to understand what quantification does, and does not, illuminate with respect to its ability to assess its own performance.

References

Astin, A. W. "Equal Access to Postsecondary Education: Myth or Reality?" *UCLA Educator*, 1977, *19* (1), 8–17.

Astin, A. W. "Traditional Conceptions of Quality in Higher Education: It's Time for a Change." Paper presented at American Association for Higher Education Conference, Washington, D.C., March 6, 1980.

Astin, A. W., and Solmon, L. C. "Measuring Academic Quality: An Interim Report." *Change*, 1979, *11* (6), 48–51.

Cartter, A. M. *An Assessment of Quality in Graduate Education.* Washington, D.C.: American Council on Education, 1966.

Clark, M. J., Hartnett, R. T., and Baird, L. L. *Assessing Dimensions of Quality in Doctoral Education: A Technical Report of a National Study in Three Fields.* Princeton, N.J.: Educational Testing Service, 1976.

Gourman, J. *The Gourman Report: A Rating of Undergraduate Programs in American and International Universities.* Los Angeles: National Education Standards, 1977.

Hughes, R. M. *A Study of Graduate Schools in America.* Oxford, Ohio: Miami University Press, 1925.

Hughes, R. M. "Report of the Committee on Graduate Instruction." *Educational Record,* 1934, *15* (2), 192-234.

Johnson, R. R. "Learning Among American Colleges." *Change,* November 1978, pp. 50-51.

Keniston, H. *Graduate Study and Research in the Arts and Sciences at the University of Pennsylvania.* Philadelphia: University of Pennsylvania Press, 1959.

Lawrence, J. D., and Green, K. C. *A Question of Quality: The Higher Education Ratings Game.* AAHE-ERIC Higher Education Research Report No. 5. Washington, D.C.: American Association for Higher Education, 1980.

Magoun, H. W. "The Cartter Report on Quality in Graduate Education." *Journal of Higher Education,* 1966, *37,* 481-492.

Morgan, D. R., Kearney, R. C., and Regens, J. L. "Assessing Quality Among Graduate Institutions of Higher Education in the United States." *Social Science Quarterly,* 1976, *57,* 671-679.

National Research Council. *A Century of Doctorates: Data Analyses of Growth and Change.* Washington, D.C.: National Academy of Sciences, 1978.

Roose, K. D., and Andersen, C. J. *A Rating of Graduate Programs.* Washington, D.C.: American Council on Education, 1970.

Judith K. Lawrence is a doctoral candidate in higher education at the University of California at Los Angeles and a research analyst at the Higher Education Research Institute in Los Angeles. She is a coauthor with Kenneth C. Green of a literature review on quality assessment studies in higher education, A Question of Quality: The Higher Education Ratings Game, *funded by the Exxon Education Foundation.*

Lewis C. Solmon is a professor in the Graduate School of Education at UCLA and HERI secretary/treasurer. He is coprincipal investigator on the HERI project to assess quality in American undergraduate education which is funded by the Exxon Education Foundation.

Most assessment efforts suffer from being externally imposed on reluctant institutions. By making the process internally designed as part of a cyclical calendar, schools — as well as outside agencies — benefit. Institutions "must negotiate some control, then do the job."

Some Theoretical and Practical Suggestions for Institutional Assessment

H. R. Kells

For ten years I have worked in institutional assessment and planning as a consultant, lecturer, and trainer on campuses and in workshops, with four of those years as a member of the staff of a regional accrediting agency. I have worked at some depth with over three hundred colleges and universities and have had contact with several hundred more as they wrestled with some kind of assessment process. The experience has been challenging and always interesting, but the overall portrait of institutional assessment which I have accumulated, along with the travel sores from over a quarter of a million miles of campus-related travel, is not an encouraging one. It is a chaotic melange more than an evolving landscape; more kaleidoscopic than impressionistic in style; and more like the graffiti of the New York subway cars than the colorful revolutionary murals on the highway underpasses of San Juan. The overall picture is frantic, troubled, and difficult to comprehend.

In this chapter I will attempt to sort out this experience; to discuss factors that appear to influence the effectiveness of the various kinds of assessment attempts, not so much in terms of definitions and classifications, as in their human dimensions, their purpose and design, and their relationship to the ongoing health and prospects for institutions. Finally, I will make some suggestions for institutions and for those who seek to impose assessment and other schemes upon the usually and, I think, understandably less than receptive campus citizens.

Although this analysis may be of interest to those from countries and institutions outside the United States—certainly some of the process suggestions may be—the bulk flows directly from the conditions created by the rather unsystematic but wonderfully diverse and responsive American "system" which has been described by Clark and Youn (1976). In contrast with the majority of other national systems, the American institutions are neither administered from the national level nor are they subject to national standards for degree structures or other aspects of institutional life. As Clark and Youn describe it, most of the power and prerogative is in the middle of the system: it is in the hands of the boards of trustees and executive leadership at the institutional level. This basic, unique condition causes a profound interest in assessing the effectiveness of institutional efforts at several levels, from many perspectives, and on the part of a large number of interests and agencies. It also causes a concatenation of demands that complicate institutional life.

Situation Today

There is no need to recount the external pressures that bombard American postsecondary institutions in this era. Similarly, we are all aware of the multifaceted and often overwhelming demands which are placed upon administrative and faculty professionals in these institutions. There is, however, a need to describe some of the characteristics of the chaotic assessment scene. It is probably most useful to examine it from various perspectives—from the standpoint of regional (multistate) and state agencies and from the standpoint of institutional leaders, program directors, and faculty members.

As most are aware, *regional* accrediting agencies are an attempt at self-regulation and self-improvement by the institutions in a particular area. They promote improvement by promoting self-assessment processes and by employing peer evaluation teams and accreditation councils, and their message is often misunderstood because of the anxiety associated with the peer review and federal fund eligibility aspects of their process (Kells, 1976; Warren, 1980). The agencies find that institutions do not seem to have much on-going assessment capacity (Kells and Kirkwood, 1978, 1979) and that any periodic, organized, participative self-assessment exercises are rarely related to a coherent, useful planning venture as part of an ongoing cycle (Kells, 1977, 1980b). These agencies often find that institutions would rather not engage in the required self-study process, but do so reluctantly and, therefore, often in an overly descriptive, mechanical, poorly led, somewhat "safe," multi-committee venture. Such a process leads to an overstuffed report. Indeed, the process too often seems to have been organized to write the report rather than to study the institution. Some changes result (Kells and Kirkwood, 1979), but the potential for broad-scale institutional renewal and useful assessment by peers is largely unfulfilled.

Reaction to the regional stimulus and review is mixed. Leaders usually tout the benefits of a peer-based process, particularly in place of a government process, and usually after it is over. Before the review, with some notable and increasingly frequent exceptions, they abhor the diversion and complain about wasted time and funds (Warren, 1980). Larger institutions with multiple accreditation relationships stagger under the weight of the system (Kells and Parrish, 1979; Pigge, 1979). The institutions usually see the self-study requirements as compounding the state-mandated study and planning requirements and any locally initiated efforts. The administrator and faculty member reactions range from "more busy work" to a deep resentment about usurping their time, which they feel is better used in teaching, other services, or research. It is easy to understand this reaction when one considers that one public university in the Northeast was recently visited *forty* times in one three-year period. Most of these visits required a prior self-assessment. All of this was in addition to state and local evaluations.

It is no surprise that as the economic situation grows worse and as state coordination boards gain power, *state* agencies have been increasing their demands that institutions study and plan, coordinate, cooperate, and evaluate almost constantly. Very little of this type of study is coordinated with institutional or accrediting schedules and most assumes that filling out forms and answering questions is the essence of assessment. Institutions grow weary and angry—aware that many of their responses to such efforts are not that useful and confident that more of the same is surely not the answer. They question simplistic assumptions and methods and what they see as the gross lack of sensitivity to the nature of academic endeavor. They react strongly—often politically—and an adversarial situation usually develops with both sides losing steadily in the resulting climate.

If administrator and faculty members react negatively to regional requests, they are often apoplectic at the state agency incursions into their work, time, and, often (as they see it), privacy. Requests are often for almost instant data and analysis of complex academic ventures. They perceive the nature of such efforts as repulsive and the methods naive and often technically incompetent. One can only imagine their reactions to reports delivered at meetings of state coordinating officials concerning the "Systematic, Coordinated, Multi-Campus Assessment (also read Planning) Effort Successfully Completed in (state)." Surely, the simple tenets of participatory, well-led, informed analysis in a social organization are rarely if ever characteristic of state-mandated efforts. Even those which are not related to institutional improvement and, some would argue, are not or cannot be participative ventures, are rarely perceived as being crisply defined and well organized, staffed, and carried out.

At the *institutional* level—more specifically regarding institutionally initiated assessment efforts—many of the conditions described above also inhere in the processes. Leaders are rarely able to sort out the demands for study and planning imposed by external sources, and they certainly have difficulty developing a local agenda for study, planning, and action amid these constant and often conflicting demands. In the absence of a strong locally initiated agenda or management philosophy and process (most academics refuse to call it this), the style is perforce reactive and wasteful. The same band of hard-working folk on the campus are dragooned into service in a seemingly never-ending sequence of studies, planning efforts, "commissions to chart the future," mission and goals efforts, management by objectives superimpositions, and program reviews. Few institutions have decided to collapse it all into a logical, cyclical sequence of locally centered study, planning, and doing. As conditions worsen and the incidence of other than improvement-oriented studies (for example, cost efficiency studies *in order* to cutback programs) increases, the prospect for establishing such control, for securing a reversal in the conditions, and for improving the nature of institutional assessment certainly grows dimmer. This is particularly so on the most hard-pressed, most vulnerable, and often (by now) totally politicized campuses. In the latter situations, it seems as if an institutional evolution occurs in which self-selection or entrapment results in a type of leadership and a cadre of professionals which defy and deny the principles of organizational health such as openness, effective communication, and ability to recognize and solve problems. These institutions are the ultimate challenge to meaningful and useful institutional assessment.

There is one other important aspect that must be addressed concerning institutionally initiated assessment efforts. It is the matter of technique and expertise. A most perplexing reality permeates almost every setting I have seen. Neither campus leaders nor other professionals—at least those drafted into service in assessment efforts—have a clear sense of how to go about their task. They have neither a usable theory nor a model which they call forth to be the basis of the effort, nor do they seem to have a reasonable level of technical expertise. They flounder searching for a system. Many grab at the first plausible approach that is suggested or that comes along at a reasonable price. They do not seem to bring the same level of professionalism to tasks like assessment or planning that they surely must apply in the pursuit of knowledge in their own discipline. This sad condition, of course, also rears its head in the other major aspects of the management role—organizing, budgeting, staffing, and training. Academic leadership is ever changing, yet with few exceptions, eternally the same.

Finally, it must be recognized that at some institutions, particularly larger, doctorate-granting institutions, the last decade has seen the tortured but generally successful evolution of systems of cyclical, sometimes improvement-oriented program reviews. These have evolved largely in response to external (or within a multi-campus system, systemwide) stimuli. In some instances, however, they have been transformed under sensitive local leadership into useful processes of assessment—linked to change and improvement and central to the life of the place. Many, however, remain isolated from ongoing useful schema, externally directed and politically skewed. Some suffer from their unfortunate primary relationship to retrenchment efforts. Some use peer visitors very badly (Kells, 1980c). (For an excellent review of such systems with a set of sound theoretical and practical recommendations, see Arns and Poland, 1980.)

So, the assessment landscape is complex and discouraging. In the pages which follow, I will attempt to put forth some suggestions that may assist in clarification of the picture and in more effective use of institutional assessment processes.

Theoretical Considerations

When going to another campus as a consultant or accepting a service role for a regional or national accrediting agency, I use a simple working construct—a complementary set of theoretical and practical postulates which form the basis of my work. They help me to clarify the chaos. They are as follows:

1. *The primary motivation of the assessment effort usually determines its effectiveness.* Basically, assessment can be internally motivated and directed, or it can be externally motivated. Both can result in some institutional improvement, but it is at least an order of magnitude more difficult in the case of response to an external stimulus. Both require that some criterion levels be set or employed which indicate worthiness or signal a problem or deficit, but in the internally motivated process these are usually locally determined and controlled by the professionals who must use the results of their determinations and who are therefore (potentially) motivated to solve any problem and implement the solution. The externally motivated study, on the contrary, often imposes criteria determined elsewhere (unfortunately, usually not predictively valid ones) which may or may not be applicable locally and therefore may or may not result in useful, constructive development at the institution. It is possible to reorient externally initiated processes to become internally motivated processes. Closely linked to the first postulate is the following one.

2. *The effectiveness of an institution should be assessed using two basic, complementary strategies — the relationship between goals and goal achievement and on how well the institution seems to function as an ongoing responsive, vital organization.* (For a full explanation of this, see Campbell, 1977, and Kells, 1980c, pp. 15-16, 63-65.) The goal-achievement studies cannot prove that the institution caused the outcomes which are ascertained, because of the lack of controls and the variation in input and intervening (external) variables (Hartnett, 1974). But if the studies are undertaken for improvement purposes, the studies can look for patterns of outcomes that should occur but do not — and then basic elements or focal points for examination, development, and change have been created. This is an absolutely critical dimension for assessors to understand. It is often misunderstood.

The second aspect (the study of how well things function) complements the first and also provides much potential for improvement in the process, environment, programming, and service aspects of our institutions. It is required because the goal-achievement studies cannot be sensitive enough to ascertain the early impact of process problems which might seriously hinder the effectiveness of the organization in a relatively short period of time.

Finally, of course, one must set usable criterion levels for each measure of goal achievement or process functioning so that the weaknesses or areas for development can be pointed out. Ideally these should be locally determined or accepted as useful.

3. *Institutions are run by people. Assessment must be accomplished by people.* This has very important implications for leadership of the process and for process design. The design of the process must match the institutional circumstances (Kells and Kirkwood, 1979), and the steps, sequences, roles, tasks, and organization of the process must be psychologically acceptable (and appropriate in terms of the leader's interests and posture). Basically, if the leader is enthusiastic and wants the process to be successful in improving the institution, it has a much better chance. The availability of useful information and a long list of other variables also affect the results of these processes, but the people-oriented and design dimensions are critical. (See Kells, 1980c.)

4. *An assessment effort must yield some strategies for and commitment to useful change.* This is the most common shortcoming I have found in reviewing hundreds of study processes, evaluation schemes, and reports thereof. Most point out or intend to point out "areas of need," "problems," or even "recommendations," but the process usually stops short of institutional commitment to change or even to study priorities, timetables, roles, and tasks. Such a process is not ongoing. There are no links to the future. It is isolated and most of the effort is wasted. (For a full examination of this question, see Arns and Poland, 1980; Kells, 1980c; Lindquist, 1978.)

Most of the foregoing is grounded in a large body of experience and some specific research studies. The references cited will provide the reader ample access to these data, case studies, and other descriptions which can be used to develop one's own set of postulates.

Practical Suggestions

What are the specific steps that institutional leaders, state agency officials, multi-campus central staff administrators, and regional and national accreditation officials can take to reduce the tangle of assessment efforts and, thereby, improve the processes, institutions, and programs to which the assessment efforts are directed? The following are offered in an attempt to assist in this regard.

1. To the maximum extent possible, *invert all externally initiated assessment efforts to become improvement-oriented, internally designed and motivated assessment efforts.* This assumes that the institutional leadership cares about improvement and is open enough to permit campus professionals to periodically and frankly assess progress in meeting goals and the way the institution functions. It also presumes that state and other external agencies, some of which have criteria to suggest or impose, do

care about institutional improvement and that they are wise enough to see that such a strategy will be much better in the long run and can meet the short-run needs of the agency. They must be sensitive, mature, and skilled enough to proceed this way. This recognizes that various criteria can be used to point to strengths and weaknesses, and that some of these may well be suggested and adopted (or adopted locally) as part of a total well-designed assessment strategy built upon studies of goal achievement and functioning. (See Campbell, 1977, and Kells, 1980a.) Even in potentially adversarial situations, an improvement-oriented strategy can be adopted and can be made to work overtime (see Arns and Poland, 1980).

To explain the potential impact of this suggestion, let us consider the case of an institution that is approached by a state or accrediting agency with the announcement that the institution's doctoral programs must be evaluated. At the very beginning of any response to such a request, the leaders of the institution face a critically important decision. Should they treat the request as merely something from an outside agency to be reacted to in a give-them-the-information-and-get-them-off-our-back process or do they decide to assess their doctoral programs using a thoughtful, internally oriented process that can produce useful suggestions for improvement and further development as well as a report for the outside agency? Internally oriented processes can yield valuable insight, political advantage through self-awareness and confidence, and improved morale. Externally oriented processes that are paste-on, partially informed, superficial, and reactive rather than proactive are always expensive (very little, if any, useful results for the funds and time invested), often yield reports which are misinterpreted, and almost always are resented by the campus participants.

2. *Vigorously establish and maintain the institution's cyclical agenda for study and complementary planning activities as the primary and controlling agenda* as opposed to a constant reactive stance. To do so will stabilize the system, maximize the return on time and dollars invested, and reduce the vast overload of study requirements to a more manageable dimension. This recognizes that institutions want to reduce such duplication (Pigge, 1979). It presumes that institutional leaders want to and can benefit from a solid, periodic cycle of study, planning, and doing, repeated with about five-year frequency (Kells, 1980b). Furthermore accrediting agencies must start to work together to accommodate basic institutional needs, and the institution (barring times of trouble or generally acknowledged dysfunction) has the right to expect coordinated self-study efforts and peer (accrediting agency) visits. These should relate to the *institution's* basic schedule for study and planning (Kells, 1980c).

This suggestion fully acknowledges that many institutions do not have a useful cyclical study and planning cycle but also acknowledges that if agencies reduce the duplication and mindlessness even 50 percent, institutions can be guided to establish such schemes, particularly if state and accrediting forces agree to such a pact. It would be insane for institutions to refuse to move to a single, vigorous, locally established schedule in favor of a continuation of the present random, duplicated overload. They must negotiate some control, then do the job thoroughly and usefully. It can yield confidence and political advantage as well as improved procedures and services. There is no free lunch in the assessment business, but it would be nice to be able to control the menu, decide that lunch can and should be served sometime between 11:00 A.M. and 2:00 P.M., and even to enjoy the food now and then.

To continue with the case of the doctoral-level institution mentioned earlier, we can best see the implication of suggestion number two by considering what will happen to the morale of the faculty members if they are asked to perform their requested assessment in addition to a self-study requirement for the regional accrediting agency and overlapping specialized accreditation reviews for several of the departments, during budget preparation, master planning, and all the other committee work for department, college or school, and university! The role of the leaders should be obvious. Courage, sensitivity, and strong leadership are needed to resist the chaos just described, but it can and should be done.

3. *Design* the process well. Start with an overview of the status of problems, goals, staff-member weariness, data, goal-achievement studies, staff turnover, informal leadership, and priorities. Build the process—its depth, breadth, participation level, steps, and sequence of activities with the foregoing in mind. Use a sequence. Use intensive rather than mindlessly protracted activities. Integrate with other assessment activities of whatever origin. Avoid heaping things on top of the pile. Train the leaders for the process. (For a thorough description of all of this see Kells, 1980c). Implicit in these suggestions is the fact that most study and planning processes are not designed at all. Committee appointments usually are made on some basis, a more or less clear charge is given, a date is set for a report, and the flag is dropped, and . . . well, we deserve what we get in these situations. (See Kells, 1977.)

Decisions must be made about whether or not to employ a work group to accomplish a task. (See Kells, 1980c, pp. 38-39; Sherwood and Hoylman, 1978.) The critical element of any group so established is the leader. Group leadership skills can be learned.

Assessment processes can be employed to make the organization function better, to have more openness and better communication, to promote problem solving, and to narrow the gap between individual and institutional goals. Useful, rewarding participative study effort promotes commitment. These things do not just happen. They result from assessment processes that are sensitively designed and skillfully managed.

The suggestion concerning design involves more subtle matters than the foregoing two. It is here that most institutions drop the ball. The dean of graduate studies or the department chairperson must spend time designing the assessment they decide to conduct or it will not run well or produce useful results. If these executives are like most of their peers, they will establish too many committees chaired by people without group leadership skills, and set them all off on an ill-defined course. The committees typically have inadequate staff help, study skills, and access to data. One thing will be clear—the date the report is due. It all smacks of amateurism and naivete, but it is the rule not the exception in educational assessment efforts. Design is needed.

4. *Include the commitment to act, develop, change, as part of the assessment process.* This means that the reports which result from such process should include agendas for action, priorities, schedules, roles, and tasks. This should be in state-initiated assessment processes as well as in the locally inspired or accreditation efforts. And here the work of Lindquist (1978) is of particular importance. The elements necessary to move a group, an institution, or an agency to change, are explained: (1) a process facilitator; (2) linkages to new ideas or information; (3) motivation and rewards from the leadership; (4) and commitment or "ownership" by the participants created through meaningful participation in the development of solutions.

The foregoing recognizes that most assessment efforts end up as unread reports on shelves or in the waste dump. It presumes that no assessment effort is useful and worth the effort unless some good comes out of it. It is frustrating enough to know a program is not doing the job, without having an unread report result from a highly touted "evaluation" or "program review." It is just as unsatisfying to fill out forms, submit documents, spend time, and host visitors to have the resulting team report provide no special insight, no suggestions for further improvement, no commitment to change—no help.

No institution will really achieve much return on the dozens of hours of internally-motivated (even though the initial stimulus was an external one) assessment work unless the designers and implementers of the process assure that suggestions for the improvement of each of the programs and for graduate work university-wide are made, discussed, decided on, and implemented as part of the process. Many of the potential fruits of the assessment process are left on the doorstep of implementation and swept away by the pressures or buried in the inertia of institutional life. An institution must take all the steps in the process if there is to be a return on investment.

So there you have it. A simple enough agenda, one which a few well-led, confident institutions have begun to pursue on a regular basis for their own benefit. It will take years to reduce the assessment morass and replace it with a simpler, institutionally based, useful, improvement-oriented, and accountable scheme. But it is worth the effort.

References

Arns, R. G., and Poland, W. "Changing the University Through Program Review." *Journal of Higher Education,* 1980, *51* (3), 268-284.

Campbell, J. P. "On the Nature of Organizational Effectiveness." In P. S. Goodman, J. M. Pennings, and others (Eds.), *New Perspectives on Organizational Effectiveness.* San Francisco: Jossey-Bass, 1977.

Clark, B. R., and Youn, T. I. K. *Academic Power in the United States.* ERIC/Higher Education Report No. 3. Washington, D.C.: American Association for Higher Education, 1976.

Hartnett, R. "Problems with the Comparative Assessment of Student Outcomes in Higher Education." Paper presented at meeting of Association for Institutional Research, Washington, D.C., May 1974.

Kells, H. R. "The Reform of Institutional Accreditation Agencies." *Educational Record,* 1976, *57* (1), 24-28.

Kells, H. R. "Academic Planning: An Analysis of Case Experiences in the Collegiate Setting." *Planning for Higher Education,* 1977, *6,* 2-9.

Kells, H. R. "Proliferation and Agency Effectiveness in Accreditation: An Institutional Bill of Rights." In *Current Issues.* Washington, D.C.: American Association for Higher Education, 1980a.

Kells, H. R. "The Purposes and Legacy of Effective Self-Study Processes: Enhancing the Study-Planning Cycle." *Journal of Higher Education,* July/August 1980b, pp. 440-447.

Kells, H. R. *Self-Study Processes: A Guide for Postsecondary Institutions.* Washington, D.C.: American Council on Education, 1980c.

Kells, H. R., and Kirkwood, R. "Analyses of a Major Body of Institutional Research Studies Conducted in the Northeast, 1972-1977: Implications for Future Research." *Proceedings* of the Northeast Association of Institutional Research, Fall 1978.

Kells, H. R., and Kirkwood, R. "Institution Self-Evaluation Processes: A Major Retrospective Analysis." *Educational Record,* 1979, *60* (1), 25-45. Also presented at Organization for Economic Cooperation and Development (OECD) meeting in Paris, France, September 1978.

Kells, H. R., and Parrish, R. *Multiple Accreditation Relationships of Postsecondary Institutions in the United States.* Washington, D.C.: Council on Postsecondary Accreditation, 1979.

Lindquist, J. *Strategies for Change.* Berkeley, Calif.: Pacific Soundings Press, 1978. (Available via the Council for the Advancement of Small Colleges, Washington, D.C.)

Pigge, F. L. *Opinions About Accreditation and Interagency Cooperation: A Nation-wide Survey.* Washington, D.C.: Council on Postsecondary Accreditation, 1979.

Sherwood, J. J., and Hoylman, F. M. "Utilizing Human Resources: Individual Versus Group Approaches to Problem Solving and Decision Making." In *The 1978 Annual Handbook for Group Facilitators.* La Jolla, Calif.: University Associates, Inc., 1978.

Warren, J. R. "Is Accrediting Worth Its Cost?" *AAHE Bulletin,* 1980, *32* (7), 11-15.

Young, K. (Ed.) *Understanding Accreditation.* San Francisco: Jossey-Bass, forthcoming.

H. R. Kells is professor of higher education and information at Rutgers University. From 1970 to 1974, he served on the professional staff of the Middle States Commission on Higher Education. He is an active consultant and researcher and runs workshops on self-study processes for several of the regional accrediting commissions.

A State University of New York program illustrates how self-assessment can serve two purposes: accreditation and sound institutional growth.

Strategies for Assessing Performance at Your Own Institution

Donald Tritschler

Modern life is so confusing there is a need for some system to evaluate available services. This need is critical in relation to higher education because one of its promises is vocational success and satisfaction. Many people do not have the personal expertise to judge a college's performance, and they turn to accreditation agencies to give a school the stamp of quality. To provide this, associations of colleges and universities became preoccupied with establishing such recognition for their members. Their accreditation began as an assurance by qualified outsiders that an institution had adequate resources and procedures — the backing, professional staff and practices, and facilities to offer acceptable programs. Recently the public has begun to ask whether these resources do indeed produce effective performance in education.

The institutional self-study was developed to answer these new questions. The institution prepares a self-study for its accreditors not only in order to establish the facts about its resources but to prove its own performance. Self-study for accreditation of curricular offerings, student learning, faculty quality, academic facilities, and administrative effectiveness becomes more elaborate as education grows more complex. Such a major effort is justified by the opportunity it offers the institution to learn about itself. Thus apologists describe the self-study as the centerpiece in a process of accreditation that works to improve education as well as validate it.

Despite the potential value of the self-study, few institutions have the confidence for complete candor with outsiders because the ultimate goal of accreditation is their recognition. If the members of the institution are wise enough to treat the self-study also as a powerful instrument for development of quality in their programs, something to which they will refer for information and insights in the future, it is more likely to be an honest document. They will not forget, however, that the self-study must culminate in accreditation.

History of Self-Assessment

In this decade the orientation of self-study has shifted from resources to performance. Hard times dictate that colleges face issues and examine their performance candidly, whether or not accreditation depends upon it. Self-study has become self-assessment. It is truly for the institutions, not just to protect their collegiate image. Through self-assessment schools seek knowledge rather than accreditation, knowledge to help make their programs attractive. Their searches are usually specific to immediate or long-range issues confronting the college. The findings must be complete and accurate or they will not be useful. If disinterested outsiders' perceptions are included, the visitors' attention will usually be directed to specific issues rather than to review of an entire institution. The integrity of institutions requires self-assessment, and so does their power to serve (Dearing, 1979).

Self-assessment as an institution's initiative in its own behalf is not without its problems. Objectivity about one's own work, especially for individuals, is difficult under any circumstances. Candor sometimes becomes impossible when the results may affect lives. Especially when the findings of self-assessment are negative, action on its conclusions is difficult. Action where it is indicated is the main justification of the effort, yet the effort of changing the status quo is easier put off than begun. As taxing as introspection alone is to the institution, it is only the beginning of the process of growth. While serious self-scrutiny is difficult to sustain, it must be a continuous process if it is to be useful over the years in helping the institution control its future.

In an experiment to test the possibility and usefulness of self-assessment, the Regents of New York encountered these and other obstacles, and also saw many of them removed. Not surprisingly the idea for self-assessment germinated in an accrediting office of the New York State Education Department, the Regents' administrative arm. The Regents have been recognized by the federal government as a national accrediting body since the Veterans' Readjustment Act of 1952 mandated that funds for veterans' education be spent only at accredited institutions. The Regents' accreditation of colleges and universities in New York, the United States, and overseas began in the late nineteenth century. Its long evolution includes most practices of the regional and the specialized accrediting bodies: published standards (Commissioner's Regulations and Regents' Rules), detailed institutional self-study, visits to campuses by academicians, and an elaborate reporting process that culminates in registration of accredited programs.

As careful as these reviews were and as detailed as was their reporting, their effectiveness depended upon circumstances beyond the control of the accreditors. Whether accreditation was accomplished by an association for one of its members, under the legal authority of the education department, or through a combined visit of the two, later evidence sometimes showed that major issues had been set aside with little action taken, even when the institution appeared to agree with the visitors on need for change. Unless the findings included such blatant breeches of standards as unqualified faculty, inappropriate curriculums, or inadequate resources, little effective action could be taken by the accreditors. When the colleges found they had to cut their budgets to survive, they were not prepared to take immediate action based on sound planning; when the necessity for cutbacks was removed, they ceased their ad hoc reviews. Attention to equally critical issues, such as unproductive programs or ineffective communication within the institution, depended upon the institution's concern for self-improvement.

These occasional disappointments led the New York Bureau of College Evaluation to propose an experiment by the colleges with self-assessment systems. The assumption was that institutions would be much more likely to act on their system's findings than on the wisdom bestowed by outsiders. Rather than the threat of mandated changes, some of which might affect individuals personally, their personal involvement in the process would show them how needed changes would be in their own interest. Institutions would be prepared to respond to external and internal forces such as inflated costs, new trends in education, or need for changes in governance or organization. The department's responsibility for accreditation might also be supported if self-assessment findings were continuously available, and the ultimate purpose of accreditation, which is support of academic quality, would be served if the findings were used (Kells, 1980).

The New York Project

In 1976 the Bureau of College Evaluation won a grant to the Regents from the Fund for the Improvement of Post-Secondary Education (FIPSE) to develop self-assessment systems in New York State. The education department would distribute small grants to colleges to experiment with models of self-assessment. The New York State Task Force on Self-Assessment, composed of these college's representatives, would attempt to establish a conviction of need for self-assessment on their campuses, develop instruments to do it, help their colleagues learn how to assess their work, and discover ways to use the findings for decision making and action. They would also test and refine broad guidelines for self-assessment which the department had drafted and would help disseminate the project's discoveries about self-assessment.

The project was announced in the first week of August. In this slow time of the academic year, forty-six schools sent representatives to an informational meeting, and thirty-one submitted proposals by September 15. Though the small size of the grant would permit funding for only nine proposals, the quality was such that when the project's national advisory council selected them for both quality and representative characteristics, they decided to ask twelve more colleges to join the project as associate members. Six of these decided to join the project without subsidy when it organized in October.

The organizational meeting established certain agreements which helped define the nature of self-assessment. While the colleges were to test models of self-assessment, their individual projects were to serve their own institutional needs first, and, second, to be designed for adaptation by others. Likewise, they were to keep the guidelines in mind but to use only those which they needed. Task Force members would attempt to establish self-assessment as a continuing practice on their campuses in order to plan and maintain quality in academic programs.

Definition. Members of the project's national advisory council further defined self-assessment as participants in the project came to understand it. Their essays which appeared in the handbook that published the guidelines and models of self-assessment analyzed it not simply as dispassionate judgment but rather as a means of getting a comprehensive understanding of programs (Dearing, 1979). It would serve as an integral part of management planning by keeping information for decision making current (Blackwell, 1979). Thus self-assessment is a continuous, objective system of monitoring educational quality which a college uses to understand and plan the development of its programs and the operations which support them.

Project Activities. The cooperation and competition within the Task Force to solve the problems they encountered in their projects helped them to develop models of self-assessment. The project held two additional Task Force meetings the first year and one the next, to which experts on evaluation were again invited to help Task Force members solve the problems they were encountering on their campuses. Another source of strength was the discussion they had with each other about mutual concerns. Finally, the prestige of FIPSE backing for the project and the department's constant interest and assistance increased the status of their self-assessment projects on their campuses.

The remainder of this chapter will examine in detail what to anticipate in assessing performance at one's own institution — the obstacles to self-assessment, ways to overcome them, procedures to accomplish self-assessment, and possible results. Some examples will be drawn from experiences with the Regents' project on Self-Assessment for Colleges and Universities.

Overcoming Obstacles

In order to establish systems of self-assessment that support growth, the institution must identify and understand the obstacles it faces. The obstacles are practical and political, but they also include conditions such as institutional inertia, or the safety of the status quo. A universal condition is the difficulty individuals and their organizations have in being objective about themselves. Another condition is lack of a dependable way to sustain an effort that is added onto what faculty and staff already do. Some feel that as professionals they already know how to evaluate their work but they nevertheless work in isolation and do not feel responsible for coping with the threats to institutional survival.

The recent circumstances of inflation, competition for enrollments, and demands for accountability from many quarters have motivated these professionals to seek systematic ways to improve their institutions. The Bureau of College Evaluation found all the expected barriers to self-assessment when it first proposed the idea in the early 1970s. By 1975, its search for likely places to experiment uncovered several colleges and universities that felt the necessity of assessments in their own behalf. In addition, the testing agencies and the higher education research centers were beginning to win acceptance of the instruments for management they had developed. The bureau nonetheless found that institutional leaders had to find incentives to encourage their campus communities to undertake self-assessment.

One strong incentive for involvement in self-assessment is major institutional support in the form of leadership and funding. If self-assessment is to result in action for change, it needs support at the highest levels—top administration and key faculty members. The chief executive officer is ultimately responsible for the effectiveness of the institution, for evaluating and planning its progress. Other officers are in a position to reward careful concern for program effectiveness and to coordinate planning in their areas. The State University of New York (SUNY) at Binghamton sees the need to link the system to budget review and long-range planning. Thus the decision makers have to be representative and have standing within the institution to win recognition for the project and cooperation on its tasks (Orlans, 1979).

One may ask if the faculty should not take initiative when self-assessment is of programs that are their direct responsibility. The response is that the process is impossible without their active participation, but their known priorities are teaching and research. They are isolated from each other and feel they cannot act appropriately on matters outside their expertise. The chief executive officer must therefore establish priority for this activity which protects the future of the entire institution. Clarkson College of Technology was especially effective in its evaluation of what its graduates need for their careers because its president held open faculty meetings on the subject, assigned key faculty to work on it, conferred informally with the trustees about progress of the project, and included a personal letter of request with the questionnaires sent to alumni and corporate employers. The first result was a basic curricular change, and the college has further plans to use the data that it collected in the surveys.

Other requirements to establish the priority of self-assessment are budgeted funds for its support and assigned responsibility for its direction. Budgeting for self-assessment not only makes it a continuous process, but availability of funds also establishes its standing. A faculty-administrative committee or a campus leader with a self-assessment advisory committee is in a position to see that the process and its results are not forgotten or left dormant. Somehow the people affected by the work of self-assessment should have prestigious representation on these committees. These representatives have a personal stake in the accomplishment of self-assessment, and their standing helps them see that it is used effectively. Binghamton went one step further to institutionalize self-assessment by appointing a faculty member to the new position of Coordinator of Evaluation.

Assignment of responsibility for self-assessment also encourages consistency in such efforts. The person or group responsible for institutional evaluation should know what efforts have been completed or are under way, so that exchange of information and techniques and coordination of findings will be mutually supportive throughout the institution. The more consistently the findings are gathered and applied, the more useful they will be on future occasions. In addition, an overview of such efforts puts the person or group in the position of an outsider who can monitor objectivity as the assessors analyze their findings about their own programs.

Often the most decisive service those responsible for self-assessment can provide for its success is their interaction with the people who must be involved in the process or with its results. Troubleshooting requires such personal contacts, but sometimes self-assessors need a dependable sounding board for their concerns, or simply encouragement from those responsible. Such interaction is also crucial when there are doubts or lack of understanding or need for adjustment of the system. Corning Community College found these contacts to be the route of several new elements in its review of administrative functions. The State University College at Plattsburgh had produced some of the project's most sophisticated data in its work on educational outcomes, but despite their elegant presentation in a report to each department, Plattsburgh's representative on the project's Task Force found the reports were not being used until she held workshops to analyze them.

Those responsible for self-assessment should help the participants establish the principles that will guide them. The ones who are affected by the findings of self-assessment and those who will do it need to agree how they will go about it, who will accomplish certain tasks, how the results will be handled, and what actions will be taken. The planners of self-assessment can focus their efforts and guide their own progress by developing a checklist.

A widely understood checklist of issues to be addressed and tasks to be completed also supports objectivity and comprehensiveness.

The guidelines that the New York project tested and published in its handbook were a framework to organize self-assessment, a series of steps one might naturally take to begin it, or a checklist for self-assessment systems already underway. A timetable is another obvious device to organize self-assessment, draw commitment of those involved, and guide their expectations of its results.

Such techniques of organizing self-assessment increase its usefulness, and so does its inclusion in a system. When Wagner College and Marymount Manhattan began developing their models of self-assessment, they found that they had histories of isolated assessments which had not been fully communicated to all who might use their findings, and which surely had not become part of a planning and decision-making process. Data needed to be organized and their collection planned in order to prepare for their distribution and use over a period of time. While other colleges' experiences with self-assessment had been good even though limited in effect, the schools tended to be discouraged by failure to get results from the long hours spent on self-assessment. They came to see the only result as one more report to file and forget, as the accreditation reports sometimes are.

One of the most effective ways to communicate the planning, progress, and findings of self-assessment, so that the idea is used, is to encourage broad involvement in it, especially of those whom it affects. A self-assessment system needs to be tuned to the political and intellectual concerns of the institution if it is to be fully supported and used (Dearing, 1979). Those persons whose support is needed for serious and decisive action on its findings must feel some ownership of the system. The groups surveyed by John Jay College of Criminal Justice about its students' curricular needs were the groups who designed the surveys. The college was even able to enlist as researchers representatives of those who doubted the value of evaluators in the reconsideration of criminal justice education. Having been on the scene from the start, these skeptics were prepared to carry out their findings and act as spokesmen for the system. The degree of others' "cooperation, and the fullness and frankness of the knowledge it yields, is vital to success, and the degree to which colleagues identify with and accept the conclusions is the final test of whether it is, indeed, a 'self' evaluation" (Orlans, 1979, p. 91).

While previous arguments have been for organizing the guidance and progress of self-assessment, the system should not upset broad involvement by interfering with the autonomy of those who must do it. It is self-assessment, after all, and one of the benefits of involving those affected by it is the special expertise and insiders' insights they bring to it. In November 1976, when New York City Community College was required to cut its budget, key faculty committees and administrators submitted their lists of evaluative measures for purposes of identifying program priorities. The lists' similarity suggested the college's leaders had identified appropriate measures, but the project was sidetracked when the fiscal pressures abated temporarily and the college went back to business as usual. When a new president arrived amid the seemingly annual budget crisis, she asked for an even broader preparation for program review based on five-year historical data for each item on an expanded list of measures. After the deans of the divisions weighted them and then reached consensus for their rank order, the results were released to the departments for further revision where necessary. The example shows broad involvement, and now the system is being used whether or not there is a fiscal crisis of the moment.

Broad involvement offers another advantage through the objectivity of multiple perspectives. While total objectivity may be impossible in self-assessment, the risk that individuals with autonomy to evaluate themselves will tend to favor their enterprises is less when interested colleagues are involved. Also, those with assigned responsibility for self-assessment have knowledge of past evaluations and are in a position to question eccentric findings or misinterpretation of accurate ones.

Gaining agreement on the meaning of self-assessment findings is sometimes difficult, but it is also another kind of opportunity to increase the system's effectiveness. Orlans (1979, p. 91) observes, "Since most institutions are divided into groups and factions. the extent of agreement about the conclusions of an evaluation attests either to their innocuousness or to an unusual sense of fraternity in the institutions." Though this wry comment implies at least some disagreement, the institution may be able to increase this elusive fraternity by maintaining involvement of people from many parts of the institution. The person responsible for self-assessment should bring these people together at several stages in its progress to exchange ideas about their mutual concern. The Task Force in New York found that their meetings and the ones they held on their campuses strengthened communication about their projects and stimulated new initiatives. The administration at the SUNY College at Oswego concentrated on involving faculty in their project, and they discovered it was a vehicle for drawing faculty and administration together.

In summary, then, of the need for broad involvement in self-assessment, what has been understood and decided on local initiative is likely to be completed effectively. People believe what they learn about themselves from self-assessment because they feel it includes their insight. Other elements necessary to overcome obstacles to self-assessment are objectivity, a sustained effort, and decisions made and used. Support from top administration and key faculty and other constituencies assures money and staff resources to sustain the effort. At large institutions, each area may be asked to contribute both money and staff, but at all institutions responsibility for completion of self-assessment must be clear.

Self-Assessment Principles

Before turning to consider procedures for self-assessment, the institution must first determine its purpose. Self-assessment may have one or more purposes, such as program improvement, economies, reorganization, market research, and accountability to others. All whose support will be needed for the system's success must be informed of its purposes and, if possible, have an opportunity to contribute. Surely those who are expected to assess themselves in earnest must help establish the goals they will have to reach. The SUNY Agricultural and Technical College at Delhi may have been exceptional in setting a policy of periodic self-assessment in response to an accreditation. Once the policy was set and the goals established, assessment mushroomed beyond academic programs to housing and other student services. Staff regarded those areas as significant programs for student development and institutional strength. For instance, the college wanted to determine what effects dormitory life had on student growth. Such goals in addition to evaluating academic programs resulted from initiatives stimulated by the college's previous successes in helping itself.

The trust to take such initiatives for self-assessment requires clear understanding of how the proposed systems will be used and by whom. Before faculty and staff begin to examine their own work, they need candid answers to their questions of how the findings will affect their careers. They need to know that they will truly share in the design, use, and benefits of the system, in order to respond with equal candor. Where will control of the system lie? How will it be shared? What implications will the findings have for personnel decisions? How will the system fit into institutional planning and resource allocation? Or will the effort be confined to a specific, nonfiscal issue? (See Peterson, 1979.)

Priorities. The priorities of subjects for self-assessment need close scrutiny because the effort expended raises the expectations of those involved in it. The issue under review not only has to be important enough among all of the institution's concerns for a follow-up on the findings but the ones who are responsible for it must make sure that its magnitude is manageable. John Jay College planned a three-tiered approach to self-assessment: "First, deal with issues having immediate and direct effect on the college—strengthen existing courses and programs; then consider matters of short-range effect (two-three years later)—study general guidelines for redesigning programs; and finally, concerns in the form of a long-range planning document for possible new programs of study" (*A Handbook for Self-Assessment,* 1979, p. 64). Marymount Manhattan found that it had to reset its priorities for self-assessment, once the many who were involved in evaluation of the college's educational services to part-time students learned what a powerful tool it was and decided to do likewise in their own areas of responsibility. Usually the priorities for assessment within a single area should be set early in the process, but they should also be subject to revision and rearrangement when necessary.

This early stage has often been called "Preassessment": through consultation, priorities for self-assessments are set, goals for each are agreed on, criteria to measure their achievement are understood. It is both a political and a practical stage. The participants establish leadership for the system and agree how they will arrive at decisions. At Delhi they reviewed their assumptions about the use and linking of staff and they anticipated the results and effects of self-assessment. Binghamton and Hofstra learned after their projects were under way that this would have been the time to be sure their goals for self-assessment were realistic. A midcourse correction of goals eventually became necessary.

This is also a time to establish principles that will keep the system on course and as effective as possible. It would be impossible to list all of the principles which could be designed to fit specific needs, but some general ones have already been mentioned. One is that self-assessment systems should operate continuously. Routine collection of longitudinal data is necessary for many planning issues. It is the only basis on which to assess change and it is the main basis for most projections. Thus self-assessment should be incorporated into campus reporting and decision-making procedures. If self-assessment is continuous, it keeps information for decision making current (Blackwell, 1979).

Self-Adjusting. A second principle is to review the self-assessment system itself. Such a review should determine the system's validity in measuring the effectiveness of the programs it examines. The assessors must consider whether the information gained is useful and the actions based on its findings are worth the human and fiscal resources expended. One expectation of self-assessment is increased understanding of the programs under review and of the reviewing system itself. Sometimes such understanding prompts changes in the reviewing system or in the program it assesses or in the planning which results from self-assessment. Self-assessment systems must be adjustable as they and their subjects become understood.

The usefulness of self-assessment increases if it includes a plan to act on the basis of its findings. Here again the assignment of responsibility is important. The person or persons responsible may need to propose a timetable to make clear to all concerned what steps are necessary and to maintain progress in their accomplishment. Such progress is a strong inducement to expend the effort necessary in self-assessment. An action plan is also an important balance to weaknesses the system uncovers. Thus the system's findings will not seem destructive; rather, its practical indications of ways to correct weaknesses will be supportive.

Depending on Data. Another principle that gains the confidence of the institution in self-assessment is to tie decisions to data wherever possible. Brooklyn College and Clarkson found the facts to be a check on hearsay. Sometimes analysis of the data leads to a major correction of the status quo. Corning Community College found that close linkage of data to decision making demonstrated the usefulness of data and helped to increase the faculty's trust in the findings of self-assessment. In addition, the focus on data will lead to more efficient self-assessment, since it will include available records and testimony of those who have relevant facts.

Self-Assessment Methods

Like the principles of self-assessment, the methods are as many as ingenuity can conceive and the demands of specific situations require. Once the principles are firmly established, the process might get under way with an inventory of past evaluations. Not only does it give those responsible a broad view of what is known and what methods have been used, both successfully and unsuccessfully, but it also helps them estimate the accomplishments of future assessments as they set their goals.

An inventory gives the assessors information on the state of self-knowledge in the institution, of the conditions and attitudes for self-assessment to be addressed, and of the preparations and further contacts that will be necessary as self-assessment progresses. The conditions and the state of knowledge at the SUNY College at Genesee led staff to begin on a small scale which expanded as the activity began to yield results and new activities were added. The task of taking the inventory itself serves the useful function of introducing the assessors and the persons and resources and interest that will be available to each other. It also offers an opportunity to involve others on campus in self-assessment from the beginning. Finally, an inventory will provide a base from which to measure the progress and results of self-assessment (Tritschler, 1977).

Another kind of record useful to those responsible for self-assessment is a log of its activities and results. This growing record of events and costs of self-assessment is useful for evaluation of the system as well as for reference when questions arise. It might include a personal account or a group's analysis of the dynamics involved in the process of self-assessment. A similar resource for understanding self-assessment is a written commentary by a participant observer to help focus the concerns of the campus on self-assessment. A portfolio of documents, events, publicity, findings, and other tangible results of self-assessment should be kept for the times when the campus wants to know where its efforts have gone.

A final, evolving record of interest especially to the managers of programs and of self-assessment systems is a planning book. A loose-leaf book of priorities, goals, objectives, policies, procedures, data, schedules, assignments, and events helps those involved in self-assessment keep current with the system (Blackwell, 1979).

Local Resources. These several records of self-assessment help make its resources on campus available to those who use it. One discovery as most colleges in the New York project took their inventories was that there were more resources available on campus than the assessors expected. Academic managers who are conditioned to seek external consultation for program reviews sometimes overlook local resources that may be superior. No doubt an outsider who specializes in performance of a specific evaluative task may bring a useful and unbiased perspective to the campus, if the task is carefully defined before hand.

However, the viewpoints of those who have a stake in the results and also those on campus who know the situation but are disinterested can often be more valuable. Plattsburgh found that interest in the data on student outcomes began to grow when the psychology department, which was familiar with such analysis, was encouraged to comment on the data.

Such consultation and other internal sources help correlate information in several areas. A representative steering committee for self-assessment has the capacity to link information built into its structure. At Clarkson the steering committee included faculty who were expert in the fields which would be necessary to direct and analyze the handling of data. This added credibility within the faculty for the committee's interpretation of the data. There are also certain sources from which assessors might especially expect to gain information. Advising and counseling programs, for instance, are not only areas to be assessed, but also a resource for information about institutional effectiveness. Binghamton established another kind of local resource, a self-assessment reading room that became a focal point for these efforts.

External Consultants. Sometimes external consultation is needed to provide information and suggest answers not available on campus, especially during the design stage of self-assessment. A technical question about collection or analysis of data, perhaps, or a skill such as management of change, or simply expert corroboration may be needed. The Polytechnic Institute of New York got guidance for development of a questionnaire about educational needs of engineers from the American Society for Engineering Education. New College of Hofstra needed a critique of its program evaluation plan when its use suggested it was too elaborate. The purposes for using external consultation should always be clearly defined, so that the consultants can gain the confidence of the campus by giving effective service. When even the experts appear to flounder, doubts about the system may arise.

Planning for Results. One of the most important preparations for self-assessment is to plan for early as well as long-range results, since results generate enthusiasm for sustained effort. Changes resulting from past evaluations at Marist College encouraged it to undertake self-assessment as an associate member of the project. Some colleges, such as Corning, may also need to plan for early action on self-assessment findings because many previous reviews have not resulted in needed changes. The system should therefore be designed to yield early or intermediate results in order to win commitment to continuous self-assessment. If findings from the first attempt do not indicate action, they may suggest new approaches or areas of self-assessment. Finally, early results or decisions protect long-range ones from premature exposure, before they are complete and confirmed.

Results of Self-Assessment

When the findings of self-assessment are ready to be used for decision making and action, they should be publicized within the institution. The effectiveness of self-assessment depends on "how well those responsible *communicate* and *educate* others about both their assessment process and its results" (Peterson, 1979, p. 96; Peterson's italics). In fact, this openness throughout the project lets all parties comment and participate, and thereby become involved in the project. When the findings are distributed, they should be accompanied by analysis and heuristic conclusions so as to stimulate discussion. Ways to achieve clear and thorough understanding of findings are to hold workshops or seminars, to discuss white papers on the subject. Such face-to-face exchanges, followed by written summaries of the meetings, overlook no areas of concern. When the entire undertaking is completed, the reporting should emphasize the results of self-assessment. The changes that occurred should be placed in an institutional perspective. Institutional change is usually a series of modest adjustments to circumstances and data which accumulate to become important initiatives (*A Handbook for Self-Assessment,* 1979).

Those who undertake self-assessment find it a means of stimulating people to think and act on what they never quite get around to doing. Its cardinal rule, involvement of those concerned with or affected by self-assessment, builds strong working relationships within the institution. Individuals find mutual concerns and new ways of supporting their own and their colleagues' interests. As people help themselves and their colleagues to find the most effective ways to accomplish their purposes, they develop confidences which "need to balance candor with discretion, honesty with charity. Self-assessment is at once a moral, political, and practical or methodological problem" (Orlans, 1979, p. 91). The evaluator must protect the confidence of those who earnestly examine their own work for the purpose of improving the institution.

Peterson sees self-assessment as one of a series of institutional practices or techniques to improve the management and the effectiveness of the institution. He recommends incorporating it with such trends as participatory democracy, political negotiation and bargaining, management information systems, simulation models and forecasting, policy analysis, planning, and staff development. No doubt the organization of self-assessment to improve programs helps keep them moving by streamlining faculty and staff decision making and putting it on a firm, factual basis.

The findings of self-assessment can be useful beyond their planned purposes. For example, they can turn external pressures for accountability into support for carefully planned priorities. Palola (1979, p. 98) outlines "the practical utility of program effectiveness studies that relate outcome and cost data": to justify budget requests, to provide information for college self-study, and to support the research of faculty committees. Study of attrition and retention of students is especially useful in reporting to institutional sponsors and to funding agencies. Mastery of information helped Corning win a grant to work on the redefinition of its mission. As self-assessment projects develop, they link with other institutional interests and sometimes illuminate them as well.

An incidental use of self-assessment findings and analysis may be for the self-study required by accreditation. Reversal of the accrediting process so that institutional information is already available before the accreditors request a self-study could make the process more efficient than it now is. Preparations for accreditation should be a simple, nearly effortless by-product of continuous systems of self-assessment. The information usually requested by the accrediting agency prior to the visit to verify what is in that self-study should already be at hand, since self-assessment is devoted to the quality of programs and much more. Indeed, some colleges and their accreditors are already developing ways for the single activity of self-assessment to serve the purpose of both accreditation and of sustaining sound institutional growth.

References

Blackwell, G. W. "The Scope of Self-Assessment in Institutional Planning: A Case Study." In *A Handbook for Self-Assessment*. Albany: University of the State of New York, 1979.

Dearing, B. "Self-Assessment for Growth." In *A Handbook for Self-Assessment*. Albany: University of the State of New York, 1979.

A Handbook for Self-Assessment. Albany: University of the State of New York, 1979.

Kells, H. R. *Self-Study Processes: A Guide for Postsecondary Institutions*. Washington, D.C.: American Council on Education, 1980.

Orlans, H. "On Institutional Self-Evaluation." In *A Handbook for Self-Assessment*. Albany: University of the State of New York, 1979.

Palola, E. G. "Program Effectiveness: Beyond Cost-Benefit Analysis." In *A Handbook for Self-Assessment*. Albany: University of the State of New York, 1979.

Comparing regional accreditation standards to research on student achievement suggests that any indirect approach to assessing institutional performance rests on a frail empirical basis.

Relationships Between Regional Accrediting Standards and Educational Quality

William E. Troutt

Obtaining and retaining regional accreditation is a rite common to most colleges and universities. The regional accreditation process represents the most universal approach to assessing institutional performance. The standards or evaluative criteria used by each of the six regional accrediting associations vary in format, emphasis, and terminology, but they share common concerns and assumptions about assessing institutional performance.

The regional accreditation approach to assessing institutional performance focuses on structure and process. Checking for the presence and adequacy of certain institutional structures and processes supposedly provides some assurance of educational quality.

This chapter discusses in more detail the results of research initially reported in "Regional Accreditation Evaluative Criteria and Quality Assurance." *The Journal of Higher Education*, 1979, *50*, 199–210.

Regional accreditation standards or criteria serve useful purposes other than quality assurance. Most standards relate to institutional self-improvement. Standards also claim to assure institutional quality, however; and in doing so, they reinforce the widely held assumption that assessing institutional performance must be done indirectly.

Academic lore has long supported the belief that institutional quality hinges on the possession of certain conditions and resources. Therefore, institutional performance could only be assessed indirectly by checking for the presence of these conditions and resources. Since many people now question this link between processes and quality, the indirect approach to performance assessment is also being scrutinized. As an extension of traditional academic thinking, accreditation practices related to the assurance of institutional quality have received considerable criticism. The following review examines regional accreditation standards in light of available research on college impact.

A review of the published standards or evaluative criteria of the six regional accrediting associations reveals eight areas of concern shared for the most part by all accrediting associations. These areas of concern include (1) institutional purposes and objectives, (2) organization and administration, (3) financial resources, (4) physical resources, (5) library/learning center, (6) student services, (7) faculty, and (8) educational program. Not all of these standards claim a direct or indirect relationship to institutional quality.

A textual analysis of published regional accrediting association standards reveals that five of the eight standards common to all associations claim some connection with quality assurance. Most regional associations say a relationship exists between institutional quality and standards for (1) institutional purposes and objectives, (2) educational program, (3) financial resources, (4) faculty, and (5) library/learning center.

These standards also serve other accreditation purposes, but accrediting associations justify them on the grounds of their relationship to institutional quality. For example, the Middle States Association sees the statement of institutional purposes and objectives as the major index of institutional quality. It views "the effectiveness of programs created to produce the results envisioned in the objectives as another index of quality" (Commission on Higher . . . , 1978, p. 4). According to Southern Association standards, "The financial resources of a college or university determine, in part, the quality of its educational program" (Southern Association . . . , 1976, p. 11). Northwest Association standards (Northwest Association . . . , 1975, p. 29) note, "In the final analysis, the performance of faculty determines the educational quality of the institution." The Middle States Association (p. 15) views the library/learning center of "paramount importance" in achieving institutional excellence. In light of the consensus that these five areas represent checks of institutional quality, the question becomes whether or not any relationship exists between these standards and institutional quality.

Regional accreditation standards assume that judgments about institutional quality should rest on inferences from certain conditions rather than direct assessment of student achievement. Regional accrediting associations defend this indirect approach to assuring quality on the grounds that a direct assessment of student performance would infringe on institutional autonomy. Requiring institutions to fulfill certain conditions and possess certain resources, however, would appear to constrain institutions far more than a check of end results.

Casey and Harris (1979) point out that the emergence of nontraditional approaches to higher education call this inferential approach to quality assurance into question. They point to findings of a recent national study of accreditation and nontraditional higher education that visiting accrediting team reports almost never deal with outcomes or results; they fail to examine assessed student achievement against the general meanings of various degrees.

Accreditation standards suggest checking the curriculum is more reliable than checking the student. Their argument equates more direct assessments of institutional quality with standardized tests. It ignores the long history in higher education of the direct assessment of student achievement by faculty.

Concerns about the outcomes of the educational process generally appear only as appendages to accreditation standards. North Central Association standards (North Central Association . . . , 1977, p. 65) state, "A direct assessment of educational and learning experiences in terms of desired outcomes should be undertaken." New England Association standards (Commission on Institutions . . . , 1976, p. 1) ask, "Does the institution have information about the postgraduate performance of its students? If so, what does this assessment suggest about the institution's programs and objectives?" Western Association standards (Western Association . . . , 1975, p. viii) indicate that "an institution is expected to provide evidence of educational outcomes in harmony with its objectives and appropriate processes." Middle States Association standards offer a plan for the measurement of outcomes. Southern Association standards call for evidence of evaluation procedures which certify the effective learning outcomes of students when member institutions submit programs at variance with standards. These statements illustrate a basic anomaly of accreditation standards:

They encourage the direct assessment of educational quality but rely on more indirect measures for assuring institutional quality.

Defining Educational Quality

Accreditation standards fail to define educational quality and assume that no common benchmarks exist for assessing institutional quality. The emphasis on checking conditions and resources betrays an unawareness or lack of concern on what quality assurance should mean in terms of student achievement. Accrediting associations suggest that imposing any common measure of institutional quality would destroy institutional diversity. All regional associations agree that institutional evaluation should be solely in terms of stated purposes and objectives. Accrediting associations refer to this relative approach to institutional assessment as qualitative. The Northwest Association (1975, p. 15) states, "Because of the diversity of institutional purposes and the processes for achieving those purposes, the standards are qualitative rather than being stated in quantitative terms." This universal dissatisfaction among the regional accrediting associations with quantitative data may grow out of the disapproval of quantitative measures that bear no relation to institutional quality. Current accreditation standards generally assume, though, that no quantitative standards or common benchmarks are acceptable.

Accrediting each institution solely in terms of the achievement of its stated purposes assumes that each institution possesses worthy purposes. According to this logic, any institution could be accredited without an assessment of the character of its goals. Accreditation attests only to the fulfillment of conditions and provision of resources necessary to make achievement of institutional goals likely.

Accreditation standards do not attribute to colleges or universities any unique functions distinguishing them from other institutions in society. Except for a statement about failure to achieve purposes, standards provide no guidance as to when an institution ceases to function adequately as a college or university. The exercise of distinguishing colleges and universities from other institutions in society points out some purposes common to all institutions of higher education. One might try to distinguish colleges and universities in terms of their basic functions. For example, assume that all colleges and universities function to provide their students with (1) a general or liberal education and (2) preparation for further study or immediate entrance into a profession or another worthy vocation. Given this assumption, accreditation could use both purposes as common tests for assessing institutional quality. Institutional environments and student populations do vary greatly, but this variation does not obviate the possibility of having all institutions judged in these two areas. Differences in institutional environment and clientele only suggest potential variations in performance criteria.

Fundamentally, regional accreditation's relative definition of quality emerges because of the lack of a commonly accepted definition of a college degree. Since the abandonment of the classical curriculum and the rise of the elective system, the meaning of a college degree has been unclear.

Like most higher education literature, publications of accrediting association standards fail to specifically define educational quality. This review assumes educational quality must relate in some way to the intellectual attainment of students. Educational quality should speak to the question of whether or not an institution's graduates can be judged as competent as their degrees signify.

Need To Validate Standards

Does any relationship exist between regional accreditation standards and evidences of educational quality? Accrediting associations fail to respond to this question with either philosophical arguments or empirical data.

The amenability of accreditation standards to empirical research presents an interesting question. Standards generally are normative statements and, therefore, not subject to empirical investigation. To say that a college ought to have a certain percentage with a doctorate represents a normative statement. Such a statement may emerge strictly out of an educator's value system. To say, however, that institutional quality hinges on a certain percentage of faculty with a doctorate represents a statement of fact. Accreditation standards divorced from claims of quality assurance might constitute normative statements. When accreditation standards involve factual assumptions, however, they become susceptible to empirical research.

It seems appropriate, then, to examine regional accreditation standards in light of available research on correlates of educational quality, to investigate whether certain institutional characteristics effect student intellectual achievement. This research does not represent a readily identifiable body of literature. Identifying such studies necessitates a review of research generally referred to as studies on college impact.

There is a vast amount of such literature. In a synthesis, Feldman and Newcomb (1969) review over a thousand studies of the effects of college on students. This large number of publications suggests the availability of a great amount of information on the relation of various college characteristics to intellectual achievement or growth. Unfortunately, only a handful of studies reviewed by Feldman and Newcomb deal with college impact on intellectual outcomes. Astin conjectures (1970) that the lack of studies of college impact on intellectual achievement results from logistical convenience. A researcher can administer psychological measures of affective outcomes easily and inexpensively to undergraduates before, during, and after college attendance.

Besides the dominance of psychological assessments of affective outcomes, college-impact studies also generally suffer from a lack of any explicit theory about the ways in which colleges produce effects on students. Feldman and Newcomb (1969, p. 211) suggest that many college-impact studies say something like the following: "Here are some interesting dimensions that may (or may not) be affected by the college experience; let's compare these variables across college-class levels. In this approach the dimensions often are measured by using existing, relatively well-validated psychological and attitudinal instruments and scales."

Astin (1977) outlines many of the methodological weaknesses of college-impact research. Much research fails to meet minimal requirements for adequately designed studies of college impact: (1) multiinstitutional data—data simultaneously collected from students at contrasting types of institutions as well as young people not attending colleges; (2) longitudinal data—information on student change between admission and a subsequent point in time. Astin notes (1977, p. 3), "Other features missing from that research include large and diverse samples of students and institutions, multiple follow-up measures of student development, including both cognitive and affective outcomes; multivariate designs for controlling differences among students entering different types of institutions; and methodological provisions for separating college effects from maturational effects or the simple process of growing up."

Despite the dominance of affective outcome studies and the methodological problems plaguing most research, this literature offers some methodologically sound studies concerned with the impact of various college characteristics on intellectual attainment. Perhaps the most useful research involves an input-output model developed by Astin and his associates. This model employs various student characteristics and college characteristics to explain outcome variations. The model enables researchers to compute an expected output based on certain student characteristics. Researchers then calculate a residual output statistically subtracting the expected output from observed student output. In turn, researchers can relate this residual output (not independent of any input characteristics) to measures of institutional characteristics and thereby determine the strength of these relationships.

This model represents an improvement over previous approaches to studying college impact, but it also receives criticism. Feldman and Newcomb (1969) point out that some portion of student outcome may result from a joint variation of student input characteristics and college characteristics. This input-output model attributes the possible joint effect of input characteristics and college characteristics solely to input characteristics.

Correlates of Educational Quality

Any research useful in determining correlates of educational quality must satisfy the following criteria: (1) employ measures of intellectual achievement or cognitive outcomes; (2) collect data from contrasting types of institutions; and (3) provide information on student change between admission and a subsequent point in time. The first criterion eliminates perhaps 95 percent of the literature of college impact, and the other two criteria rule out most of the rest. Only the following four studies survive this screening process.

In one of the earliest college-impact research efforts, Learned and Wood (1938) administered comprehensive achievement tests to nearly 45,000 Pennsylvania students. This research involves successive achievement examinations of the 1932 college generation in 1928 (upon leaving high school), in 1930 (at the close of the sophomore year), and in 1932 (at graduation). The study finds that no relationship exists between the amount of student exposure to an educational program and tested student achievement. To illustrate their findings, Learned and Wood note that basing graduation at one Pennsylvania college on intellectual attainment rather than accumulated credits would produce radically different results. The graduating class would consist of 28 percent seniors, 21 percent juniors, 19 percent sophomores, and 15 percent freshmen. Each contingent represents roughly one fourth of the new class. This study's major weakness lies in its failure to separate the effects of different college characteristics from effects potentially attributable to maturation or student ability at college entrance. Interestingly, the study concludes (Learned and Wood, 1938, pp. 68-69) with the following commentary on accreditation standards: "What degrees do teachers have? How much are they paid? What is their 'load'? . . . The physical plant must also be 'checked' . . . what clearly results from this mass of variables is a uniform mask or pattern under which . . . almost any sort of individual minds may be concealed. It is an impossible game with artificial counters. The student who is both chief player and the sole stake in the process is ignored by the rules. He wins or loses by imaginary score."

Nichols (1964) examines student academic growth in terms of Graduate Record Examination (GRE) Aptitude Test performance. In this study, scores of the National Merit Scholarship Qualifying Test (NMSQT) serve as a control for differences in academic ability prior to college. Nichols' study includes a sample of 356 students at ninety-one colleges. Nichols predicts GRE Aptitude Test scores based on college entrance examination scores and subtracts these predicted scores from actual GRE Aptitude Test scores to obtain scores independent of initial student characteristics. His results show institutional characteristics such as faculty-student ratio, library books per student, ability level of the student body, and college affluence unrelated to changes in academic performance.

Nichols' study suffers some important limitations. In addition to its small size, the sample includes only students taking the NMSQT. The use of a general aptitude test rather than an achievement test further limits the usefulness of the study.

Astin (1968), in a later study of student academic growth, also uses the NMSQT as a measure of academic ability prior to college. However, he more appropriately uses as output measures the GRE Area Tests (general college-level achievement tests in the areas of social science, humanities, and natural science). Astin uses the previously mentioned input-output model to arrive at scores independent of any input characteristics. The study involved undergraduates attending thirty-eight institutions, mostly liberal arts colleges, representing both rich and poor as well as selective and unselective institutions. Astin concludes that traditional indexes of institutional quality—a large library, high expenditures per student, a highly trained faculty, a low faculty-student ratio, and selective admissions policy—do not appear to contribute to student achievement. Astin presents a methodologically sound study, but a relatively small sample limited to students taking the NMSQT prior to college restricts his study.

Rock, Centra, and Linn (1970) report different results in a study of the relationship between college characteristics and student achievement. Their study involves a sample of 6,855 students from ninety-five colleges. This research also uses GRE Area Tests as the measure of academic achievement but employs the Scholastic Aptitude Test (SAT) to control for differences in student academic ability at college entrance. Researchers use an input-output model to arrive at scores independent of input characteristics. Unlike previous research, this study finds a small but significant relationship between student achievement and two college characteristics, college income per student and the proportion of faculty with the doctorate.

This study's shortcoming lies in the sampling of participating institutions. Of the ninety-five institutions sampled, only ten enroll over 2,000 students and only four represent state colleges or universities. The sample hardly represents all of American higher education.

Several studies failing to meet the earlier listed criteria relate in some way to correlates of educational quality. Knapp and Goodrich (1952) identify certain types of institutions as highly productive by using graduate attainment of advanced degrees and other awards as criteria for institutional quality. Later studies by Holland (1957), Thistlethwaite (1959), and Astin (1961) find that differences in institutional productivity disappear with adjustments for the abilities, talents, and goals of students. Some studies of college effects such as those by Jacob (1957), Lehman (1963), and Chickering, McDowell, and Campagna (1969) find little or no relationship between student change and college characteristics. Several early college-impact studies report changes in scores on various measures of intellectual performance, but they fail to provide multi-institutional data for institutional characteristic comparisons.

In his study of the relative quality of graduate departments, Cartter (1966) finds that library resources and faculty salaries correlate with quality ratings, or prestige relative to other institutions. A study of the quality of doctoral programs by the Educational Testing Service (1976) concludes, though, that high ratings on indicators of quality such as reputation, physical and financial resources, and faculty publications will probably mean lower ratings on indicators of quality such as student satisfaction and ratings of teaching and the learning environment.

The findings of two major studies focusing on the relationship of elementary and secondary school resources to student achievements are consistent with the general conclusions emerging from the literature on college impact. In a massive search that included 1,170 high schools and 3,233 elementary schools, one study (Coleman and others, 1966) reports a strong relationship between student achievement and the educational backgrounds and aspirations of other students. These writers find that school resources have little effect on student achievement. Another large study (Jencks and others, 1972) of the relationship of background factors and school resources to student achievement finds that no school resource or policy bears a consistent relationship to effectiveness in increasing student achievement. This study concludes that "the character of a school's output depends largely on a single input, namely, the characteristics of the entering children. Everything else—the school budget, its policies, the characteristics of the teachers—is either secondary or completely irrelevant" (p. 96).

Standards

Five quality assurance standards for regional accreditating associations were identified earlier. Research on correlates of educational quality addresses each in the following ways.

Institutional Goals. The clarity of institutional purposes and objectives and the degree to which various constituencies understand them represents one index of institutional quality according to regional accreditation standards. The Middle States Association holds (Commission on Higher . . . , 1978, p. 4), "The major index of an institution's quality is the astuteness with which it has defined its tasks." Unfortunately, no research exists to confirm or deny this claim. Only two studies even remotely relate to institutional quality and institutional purposes and objectives. In a study of college impact on affective student outcomes at thirteen liberal arts colleges, Chickering and his associates find no support for the notion that small liberal arts colleges with distinctive purposes and orientation produce more change in students than less distinctive institutions. In a major study of college and university goals, Gross and Grambsch (1968) note a strong relation between prestige (a popular image of quality) and certain types of institutional goals. Their study does not address institutional quality in terms of student attainment, however, or the clarity of goals or purposes.

Educational Programs. Educational program adequacy represents another accrediting association quality check. Educational programs must be congruent with institutional purposes and contain a certain amount of general education. Limited research fails, however, to confirm a relationship between educational program differences and student achievement.

Learned and Wood's massive study of Pennsylvania college students finds no correlation between educational programs and student achievement. In view of these results, Learned and Wood (1938) call for a new approach to educational programming based on student attainment rather than exposure to the curriculum. College-impact research on affective outcomes also fails to establish a relationship between student change and different types of educational programs. For instance, Jacob (1957) finds little significant change in student values attributable to curriculum. Likewise, Lehman (1963) reports that informal, nonacademic experiences seem to produce the most change in student affective outcomes.

Financial Resources. Accrediting associations also view financial resources as a determinant of institutional quality. Standards ask for evidence of financial stability, but define financial stability solely in terms of resources necessary to carry out institutional purposes. Limited research on the relation of financial resources to educational quality produces inconclusive results.

In his examination of student academic growth in terms of GRE Aptitude Test performance, Nichols (1964) finds no relation between academic growth and college affluence. In a similar study using GRE Area Tests as performance measures, Astin (1968) concludes that high expenditure per student does not appear to contribute to student achievement. In another study using GRE Area Tests as measures of achievement, Rock, Centra, and Linn (1970) report a small relationship between student achievement and college income per student but no relationship between achievement and college per student expenditures.

Faculty. Accrediting associations indicate that faculty qualifications represent another significant check of institutional quality. Accreditation standards uniformly state that faculty preparation and experience must be such as to further institutional purposes. Available research provides differing results on the relationship of faculty qualifications to educational quality.

Nichols' 1964 study fails to test the relationship between faculty credentials and educational quality, but he does note the lack of a relationship between student-faculty ratio and student academic performance. Astin (1968) finds measures of student achievement unrelated to either a highly trained faculty or a low student-faculty ratio. A 1970 study by Rock, Centra, and Linn, however, does report a small but significant correlation between student achievement and the proportion of faculty with the doctorate.

Library/Learning Center. All regional accrediting associations note the importance of the library as a benchmark of institutional quality. Standards do not specify minimal library size, but they do indicate library resources must adequately support institutional programs. Available research demonstrates no relationship between differences in library resources and student achievement.

Nichols' research (1964) uncovers no relation between library books per student and changes in student academic performance. Astin (1968) also fails to find a relation between library size and academic outcomes. Rock, Centra, and Linn likewise discover no relationship between student achievement test performance and either the total number of library books or the number of library books per student. Cartter's study of departmental rankings (1966) represents the only literature showing a correlation between any measure of institutional quality and differences in library resources. Cartter bases his research, however, on perceived prestige rather than measures of academic performance.

Weaknesses of Accreditation

The preceding review suggests available research cannot substantiate the claim that certain accrediting association standards assure institutional quality. It also illustrates, however, the difficulty in authoritatively stating that research demonstrates the lack of any relationship between accrediting association standards and institutional quality. This test of accreditation standards by available research suffers from three major weaknessess.

First, the small number and inherent limitations of the studies involved makes this review inconclusive. Four studies hardly represent a definitive examination of American higher education, especially four studies limited in their sampling either by type of institution, type of student, number of students, or geography. Second, the examinations used to measure academic performance further limit the interpretation of research results. A test of intellectual aptitude, such as the one employed by Nichols, measures relative ability rather than achievement. Even achievement tests, however, represent limited measures of educational quality. The two achievement tests used in these studies measure only the broad general outcomes of education and do not reflect the distinctive curricular emphasis of individual institutiona. Third, substantiation of accreditation standards does not represent the initial purpose of these four studies. These studies view institutional characteristics, such as number of library books, in terms of highs versus lows rather than acceptable versus unacceptable. Ideally, a study designed to substantiate accreditation standards might more appropriately focus on institutional characteristics of accredited institutions and achievements of their students versus institutional characteristics of nonaccredited institutions and achievements of their students. Unfortunately, the limited number of unaccredited institutions makes such a study unlikely.

This chapter does point out the frail empirical basis upon which accrediting association standards rest. It also illustrates the difficulties in substantiating any indirect approach to assessing institutional performance. It should not, however, be interpreted as primarily an indictment of regional accreditation standards.

Accrediting association standards, like all social policies, express both the virtues and the problems of the social units they represent. The deficiencies of current regional accreditation standards represent the shortcomings of American higher education. Since the demise of the classical curriculum, American colleges and universities have delegated final authority for assuring graduate quality to academic accountants (registrars). Students graduate on the basis of completing a prescribed number of courses rather than direct assessments of performance. Graduation requirements represent time served but not necessarily attainments earned. Current regional accreditation standards support a time-served approach to degree requirements and assume graduate quality can be inferred from the character of experiences a student receives.

Regional accreditation standards at the turn of the century dealt directly with quality concerns by insisting on minimal standards for college admission. The disappearance of the classical curriculum a few years earlier prompted a need for criteria to distinguish institutions providing college-level work from those offering primarily preparatory instruction. An accreditation standard checking admissions requirements helped make this distinction. Regional accrediting associations long ago discontinued, however, any standard regarding specific admissions requirements. Higher education's current egalitarian commitment makes a renewed focus on admissions standards unlikely.

Regional accreditation standards never required exit standards for students. With a few notable exceptions, performance standards for graduation disappeared from higher education with the classical curriculum.

In moving to a more direct approach to assessing institutional performance, the focus should be upon student performance at graduation. Institutions need to become very explicit in describing the learning outcomes expected for the degrees they award. Assessing institutional performance then becomes a matter of checking demonstrated student achievement against the descriptions of degrees awarded. Moving to this more direct approach brings its own set of challenges, but the current indirect approach to assessing institutional performance leaves higher education with an embarrassingly unsubstantiated means of assuring quality.

References

Astin, A. W. "A Re-examination of College Productivity." *Journal of Educational Psychology*, 1961, *52*, 173-178.
Astin, A. W. "Undergraduate Achievement and Institutional 'Excellence.'" *Science*, 1968, *161*, 661-668.
Astin, A. W. "The Methodology of Research on College Impact." *Sociology of Education*, 1970, *43*, 223-254, 437-450.
Astin, A. W. *Four Critical Years: Effects of College on Beliefs, Attitudes, and Knowledge.* San Francisco: Jossey-Bass, 1977.
Cartter, A. M. *An Assessment of Quality in Graduate Education.* Washington, D.C.: American Council on Education, 1966.
Casey, R. J., and Harris, J. W. *Accountability in Higher Education: Forces, Counterforces, and the Role of Institutional Accreditation.* Washington, D.C.: The Council on Postsecondary Education, 1979.
Chickering, A. W., McDowell, J., and Campagna, D. "Institutional Differences and Student Development." *Journal of Educational Psychology*, 1969, pp. 315-326.
Coleman, J. S., and others. *Equality of Educational Opportunity.* Washington, D.C.: U.S. Government Printing Office, 1966.
Commission on Higher Education of the Middle States Association of Colleges and Schools (CHE-MSACS). *Characteristics of Excellence in Higher Education.* Philadelphia: CHE-MSACS, 1978.
Commission on Institutions of Higher Education—New England Association of Schools and Colleges (CIHE-NEASC) Inc. *Standards for Membership-Institutions of Higher Education.* Burlington, Mass.: CIHE-NEASC, 1976.
Educational Testing Service. *The Assessment of Quality in Graduate Education: Summary of a Multidimensional Approach.* Princeton, N.J.: Educational Testing Service, 1976.
Feldman, K. A., and Newcomb, T. M. *The Impact of College on Students.* San Francisco: Jossey-Bass, 1969.
Gross, E., and Grambsch, P. V. *University Goals and Academic Power.* Washington, D.C.: American Council on Education, 1968.
Holland, J. L. "Undergraduate Origins of American Scientists." *Science*, 1957, *126*, 433-437.
Jacob, P. E. *Changing Values in College: An Exploratory Study of the Impact of College Teaching.* New York: Harper & Row, 1957.
Jencks, C., and others. *Inequality: A Reassessment of the Effect of Family Life and Schooling in America.* New York: Basic Books, 1972.
Knapp, R. H., and Goodrich, H. B. *Origins of American Scientists.* Chicago: University of Chicago Press, 1952.
Learned, W. S., and Wood, B. D. *The Student and His Knowledge.* New York: The Carnegie Foundation for the Advancement of Teaching, 1938.
Lehman, I. J. "Changes in Critical Thinking, Attitudes, and Values from Freshman to Senior Years." *Journal of Educational Psychology*, 1963, *54*, 305-315.

Nichols, R. C. "Effects of Various College Characteristics on Student Aptitude Test Scores." *Journal of Educational Psychology,* 1964, *55,* 45–54.

North Central Association of Colleges and Schools—Commission on Institutions of Higher Education (NCACS-CIHE). *Handbook on Accreditation.* Boulder, Colo.: NCACS-CIHE, 1977.

Northwest Association of Schools and Colleges—Commission on Colleges (NASC-CC). *Manual of Standards and Guide for Self-Study.* Seattle: NASC-CC, 1975.

Rock, D. A., Centra, J. A., and Linn, R. L. "Relationships Between College Characteristics and Student Achievement." *American Educational Research Journal,* 1970, *7,* 109–121.

Southern Association of Colleges and Schools (SACS). *Standards of the College Delegate Assembly.* Atlanta: SACS, 1976.

Thistlethwaite, D. L. "College Environments on the Development of Talent." *Science,* 1959, *130,* 71–76.

Western Association of Schools and Colleges (WASC). *Handbook of Accreditation.* Oakland, Calif.: WASC, 1975.

William E. Troutt is executive vice-president of Belmont College, Nashville, Tennessee.

Colleges and universities in both Europe and North America are experiencing financial shortages and changing needs. Under these conditions, direction for the future must come from faculty and administrators, not outside managers.

European Perspectives Suggest Other Criteria

John Sizer

Many institutions of higher education in Western Europe and North America have entered, or are entering, a period of financial stringency, falling real income per student, and perhaps actual decline in student numbers during the remainder of this century. They are increasingly being asked to justify their activities and account for their use of resources in terms of their effectiveness and their efficiency, not only to external financing bodies but also to other influential groups in society. Reimut Jochimsen (1979, p. 7), minister for Education and Science, North Rhine Westphalia, Federal Republic of Germany, reflected the prevailing view of such groups in many Western European countries when he argued that "as a consequence of the loss of central esteem for progress, growth, and consensus within society, the higher education sector is in danger of being stamped as a steady drain on public resources." Furthermore, within institutions, consideration has to be given to the efficiency of the various academic and service departments, decisions made concerning the allocation of resources, in some cases involving major cutbacks and reallocations. Managements need a sound basis upon which to arrive at and justify such decisions; in particular they need to develop and employ appropriate methods for allocating resources and for assessing the performance of the component parts of their institutions. Inevitably, there is a demand for performance indicators that will aid (and possibly oversimplify) this process and for relevant financial, quantitative, and qualitative information for planning, decision making, and control.

In the United Kingdom, institutional performance assessment has to be undertaken against the background of the long-term demographic trends (Department of Education and Science, 1978, 1979); the requirement to charge overseas students full economic fees; an emerging policy focus and reorganization within the Department of Education and Science designed to achieve a capacity to plan a rationalization of further and higher education as a whole; short-term pressures to reduce the level of government expenditure on higher education; and considerable uncertainty as to the level of long-term resource provision. Similar factors appear to be operative throughout Western Europe. Within institutions there is a need to balance the pressure for increased cost efficiency and possible restrictions on student admissions in the short term with the actions that need to be taken if institutions are to be effective in the long term.

Various aspects of institutional performance assessment have been considered elsewhere (Sizer, 1979a, 1979b, 1979c, 1980a, 1980b). This chapter examines the changing nature of institutional performance assessment under conditions of financial stringency, possible contraction, and changing needs.

What do we understand by the term *institutional performance assessment?* Is it concerned with the measurement or observation of the effective and efficient accomplishment of the expectations of the institution's constituencies (Romney, Bogen, and Micek, 1979)? Is it an examination of the objective achievement process, which consists of at least four distinct stages in which objectives are set, resources are committed for the purpose of achieving these objectives, committed resources are expended to achieve the objectives, and outcomes result (Romney, Gray, and Weldon, 1978)? If it is, should indicators of performance be viewed in this context and is the setting of long-term objectives for institutions the most critical stage at the present time?

Partial Performance Indicators

At the General Conference of the Institutional Management in Higher Education (IMHE) Program in 1978 it was argued (Sizer,

1979b) that given the complexities and difficulties surrounding the objective-setting and planning process, and the difficulties associated with nonprofit performance evaluation techniques and multidimensional analysis, it is not surprising that there is a tendency to recognize those parts of the institution that can be measured and monitored with a considerable degree of precision. While it may not prove possible to agree on objectives, measures outcomes, and develop performance indicators for an institution as a whole, it often proves possible to do so for parts; it is possible to develop performance indicators that relate physical and monetary inputs to physical and monetary outputs and outcomes, and to build these into the planning and reporting system.

The objectives and properties of various service performance indicators were considered (Sorenson and Grove, 1977) and from these, partial performance indicators for institutions of higher education were identified. (Sizer, 1979b, offers a matrix that plots focus of measure—such things as availability, appropriateness, effectiveness, and outcomes/benefits/impacts—against conceptual content and indicated results.) Many of these partial performance indicators are traditional process measures of institutional performance, such as staff-student ratios and cost per FTE, rather than outcome measures or ones that substantiate progress toward achieving objectives. Traditional process measures of institutional performance were widely rejected by respondents in a survey by Romney (1978) of institutional goal achievement in forty-five American colleges and universities. Objective measures pertaining to impacts of higher education such as satisfaction, ability to apply knowledge, publications, and value added were most preferred.

No doubt Romney's respondents (faculty, trustees, and administrators) would argue that if an effective institution of higher education is one which achieves objectives which are appropriate to the environment in which it operates, its effectiveness should be measured in terms of outcomes/benefits/impacts of its teaching and research programs on society. There is a danger in using short-term input indicators of performance that sight might be lost of the long-term measure of the effectiveness of institutions, that is, their contributions to the needs of society. Furthermore, questions concerning the quality of outcomes and their impact on society are bound to be raised by governments determined to get better value for public expenditures in higher education. In other words, short-term quantitative input and outcome measures and performance indicators are inadequate, and quality of outcomes and long-term impacts or benefits should be assessed. Thus, if the management

Table 1. Properties of Performance Indicators in Higher Education

Focus of Measure	Conceptual Content	Tells	Examples
Availability	Amount and type of course, research facility, or central service provided	What can be obtained	List of services available in Careers Advisory Service; list of research facilities and opportunities available in academic department; number, capacities, and locations of lecture and seminar rooms.
Awareness	Knowledge of User Population of existence; range and conditions for entry or use of courses, research facilities, or central services	Who knows about what is available	Knowledge of prospective students of courses offered by an academic department. Knowledge by prospective users of services provided by central computer center.
Accessibility	Indicates if services can be obtained by appropriate groups	Ease of reaching and using facility	Availability of photocopying facilities; location of parking lots; average waiting time for literature search by library information service; opening hours of medical center.
Extensiveness	Compares quantity of services rendered with capacity available and/or potential demand	"How Much" but not "How Well"	Students enrolled in courses compared with course quotas; number of users of library; clients in medical center; percentage of final year students using Careers Advisory Service; percent utilization of lecture and seminar rooms.
Appropriateness	Correct type and amount of service rendered, course offered, or research undertaken	Is quantity and/or quality of facility offered that required?	Demand for courses: number and quality of applicants; mis-match between computing facilities required and available; comparison of class sizes to lecture and seminar room capacities.

Efficiency	Compares resource inputs with outputs	How much resource was used such as • How much did it cost per unit? • How much did it cost in total? • How much time did it take? • What grade of employee was used?	Cost per client service in medical center. Cost per FTE student by course. Cost per literature search. Cost per meal served.
Effectiveness	Compares accomplishment with objectives (or what was intended) • Qualitative • Comparative	Characteristics; Duration; Content; Effect; Proportions served; Variances from Budgets, standards	Comparison of planned with actual: percent utilization of lecture and seminar rooms; number of students graduating; number of graduates employed; ratio of actual utilization to planned utilization of computer; comparison of budgeted cost of central service with actual cost; comparison of actual cost of FTE for course with planned cost; comparison of planned course content with actual course content; actual wastage rate compared with planned wastage rate.
Outcomes/Benefits/Impacts	Identifies Social or Economic Benefit	Monetary effects Non-monetary effects	Increase in earnings arising from attendance at/graduating from course; benefits to society of successful research into previously incurable disease; benefits to local community of cultural program; patents and copyrights registered.
Acceptability	Assess match of service/course/research outcomes with user/participant preferences	User satisfaction with services; Student satisfaction with courses; Client satisfaction with outcome of sponsored research	Demand for courses; number of complaints to librarian; course evaluation at end of lecture program; repeat sponsoring of research.

of retrenchment is to preserve excellence, there must be some way to obtain quality assessments and use them for making selective priority decisions (Balderston, 1979).

This argument is fine and logical but the difficulties involved in developing impact/benefit/outcome measures, and incorporating them into management information systems, should not be underestimated. It is likely that highly sophisticated research designs will be required, which not only will prove expensive but will involve a degree of complexity that may be regarded as impractical, probably rightly so, by administrators. The fact is that the art of measuring the outcomes remains in a distinctly primitive state, and we do not know how to measure the quality of institutional research and community-service outcomes (Romney, 1978). Nevertheless, it may well be that the time is right in many countries to attempt to assess the quality of institutions and the social value of different disciplines.

It is not surprising that during the expansionary 1970s administrators and decision makers tended to fall back on quantitatively based process measures even though they know these are inadequate measures even though they know these are inadequate measures of institutional effectiveness. Admittedly many of these measures (such as staff-student ratios and cost per FTE) are relevant to decisions regarding internal planning, control, and resource allocation, and for measurement of efficiency as opposed to effectiveness. As Delany (1978, p. 388) has pointed out, the function of control "does not cover other aspects of policy making which deal with the quality of outputs." It is concerned with the relationship between expected and actual inputs and expected and actual outputs.

Romney (1978) believes institutions should concentrate, for the purposes of assessing institutional effectiveness, upon the development of measures that substantiate progress toward achievement in those few goal areas that constituencies consider appropriate. The author believes there is a strong case for developing progress measures of performance in addition to process measures and measures of outcomes/benefits/impacts.

Future Needs

Despite Romney's view (1978) that much research is needed regarding the translation of institutional goals into measurable, observable objectives, there is considerable pressure in many European countries for a concerted effort to be made to develop and obtain agreement within institutions on their academic policy and objectives for the 1980s and into the 1990s. In looking forward in response to demographic trends, should not institutions examine the environment in which they will be operating and attempt to identify what the needs of society will be? Inevitably, it will be argued that we are not very good at forecasting the future needs of society, but surely it is better to attempt to identify and satisfy future needs than to assume in a rapidly changing society that today's needs (frequently measured in terms of number and quality of applications from school leavers) are the best and only indicators we have of future needs. Furthermore, it is often argued in the United Kingdom that because we cannot plan very effectively in the short term at the present time, there is little point in attempting long term planning. This argument confuses problems arising from short-term financial uncertainties with the need to examine the impact of long-term trends on an institution's portfolio of activities and to develop a strategy for the institution's long-term development.

Consideration of the current and future factors which are significantly influencing the environment in which institutions of higher education will be operating (Sizer, 1980b) indicates that it is not simply a question of examining the impact of falling numbers on the higher education system, but that it is also necessary to recognize that society is likely to require a different mix of outputs from the system than at present. Thus Jochimsen (1979, pp. 7, 8) argued that while "a policy directed towards both preserving, and making the necessary improvements to, the standards of efficiency at universities can be implemented only if members, professors, administrators, and students join in a new effort"; an essential precondition for such an effort is that "policy makers and society in general can really be convinced that such higher education institutions are not only willing to fulfill, but are also capable of fulfilling, the tasks required of them from the societal aspect."

If we accept Jochimsen's arguments, a key question is: who provides the scenario documents which attempt to identify the "tasks required from a societal aspect?" Clearly, government departments and agencies should undertake macroforecasting as a basis for decisions about higher education systems. They can provide scenario documents for use by institutions, but in the end should each institution form its own view and discuss this with the appropriate financing body? Once financing bodies go beyond the provision of scenario documents, questions concerning the autonomy of universities will naturally be raised; though the IMHE Programme State of the Art Survey (Institutional Management . . . , 1980) and the AUPELF/IMHE study of financing and control systems (Hecquet and Jadot, 1978) show that institutional autonomy has been considerably eroded already in a number of European countries. Furthermore, many financing bodies may not have the expertise or resources to provide scenario documents, and some governments are averse to new initiatives which necessitate public expenditure. Nor, given the difficulties involved in preparation, should we think in terms of a single agreed scenario. If they can be mobilized, the expertise and resources required to develop scenario documents are likely to be available within institutions. As the Committee of Vice-Chancellors and Principals in the United Kingdom has argued: "Forty-five universities, each making its own informed interpretation of national needs, may well, between them, arrive at several valid versions of the best long-term pattern of research and teaching while the inevitable mistakes will not be on the grand scale of government miscalculations" (1980, p. 8). Institutions have to decide whether to develop their own scenarios. If they do not there is a danger that excessive weight will be given to historical data and inadequate consideration to the changing needs of society when making selective priority decisions. Furthermore, if policy makers cannot be convinced that institutions are willing to respond to the needs of society, they are likely to opt for a more interventionist approach toward higher education; there are clear signs that many governments are developing more explicit approaches which further threaten institutional autonomy.

Certainly a consideration of the trends in society which are likely to impact upon higher education highlights the need for institutions to recognize that they must plan not only for declining numbers but also for the need for resource mobility on the one hand and for research in anticipation of new course demands, research and consultancy opportunities, and services to the community on the other. It may also be necessary to meet the needs of new groups of participants and new patterns of attendance may be required to meet individual needs. Therefore, should the performance of an institution be assessed in terms of its responsiveness to these changing needs of society and appropriate performance indicators be developed to measure an institution's progress in developing and implementing its strategy for resource mobility and responding to these changing needs?

Portfolio Analysis

One starting point in the process of responding to changing demands is to analyze an institution's historical and current performance. If such an analysis is combined with a continuous examination of the future environment to identify society's needs, it should initiate a consideration of whether the institution should market existing courses and research facilities more effectively in existing markets, consolidate others, withdraw certain courses from the market, market existing courses and research and physical facilities in new markets, develop new courses and research facilities for existing markets, or develop new courses and research facilities for new markets. Such an exercise would ultimately lead the management of the institution to identify its critical resources and to ask which is the appropriate strategy, given its current and anticipated future resources; it should stimulate institutional self-evaluation.

Thinking along similar lines, Doyle and Lynch (1979) of the University of Bradford Management Center, have applied the product portfolio concepts developed by the Boston Consulting Group (Hedley, 1976, 1977) to the analysis of a university's competitive position. They have modified the Boston group's planning matrix (Figure 1) to plot market size against market share to distinguish four types of courses:

Prop. (The Boston Consulting Group calls these "cash cows.") A prop is a big share of a small market. Doyle and Lynch consider such courses good for the university's reputation, but there are limited opportunities for expansion without a sharp decline in entry standards.

Dogs. These courses are in small areas nationally, and the university get a small share of those applying. It is suggested that such courses are not a good use for the university's small resources and consideration should be given to phasing them out in the long run.

Problem Areas. (The Boston Consulting Group describes these as "question marks.") These degree areas are strong nationally, but the

Figure 1. University Course Portfolio

	MARKET SIZE	
	Big	Small
MARKET SHARE — Big	STAR	PROP
MARKET SHARE — Small	PROBLEM AREA	DOG

university's own courses are relatively unattractive to applicants (big market, small share). The general problem is a weak reputation in an attractive area for expansion. Doyle and Lynch suggest often the problen is caused by a university proliferating its courses too widely and not concentrating in areas of greatest opportunity. If these courses are to be successful, they suggest the university must give them a major investment priority to build up staff, research, and support services, If, however, it has many courses in this quadrant there is almost certainly a case for rationalization.

Stars. These are the university's strongest courses: in areas attracting a large number of applicants and where it has a strong reputation. Doyle and Lynch consider, in general, the university should give the highest priority to supporting the strength and reputation of departments offering these courses, and they should attract a disproportionate share of new resources.

Doyle and Lynch argue that the model offers university administrators a tool to assess demand implications and test the viability of alternative strategic priorities. Of course, they would accept that an analysis of an institution's current course portfolio is only a starting point in determining future strategies. Not only is it necessary to forecast future market growth rates to determine whether, for example, today's props will become tomorrow's dogs, but also to assess the institution's critical resources to determine whether these can be employed to develop star positions in emerging areas. By substituting market size in their matrix for market growth rate in the Boston matrix, Doyle and Lynch do not differentiate between high growth, low growth, and declining markets. Their model is attractive in that it relates courses to markets, but it is a static one. Resources tend to attach to subject areas not courses, and by concentrating on subject areas, account can also be taken of research, scholarship, and community service. Therefore, in assessing a university's performance potential, do we need to compare a university's strengths in various subject areas relative to other institutions with the future attractiveness of subject areas so as to identify priority areas for future growth, consolidation, and rationalization? Such an analysis might provide a starting point for internal discussions on the institution's long-term strategy for resource mobility.

The policy directional matrices employed by General Electric (Allen, 1978) and by the Shell Group (Robinson, Hichens, and Wade, 1978) have been adapted for higher education by measuring Subject Area Attractiveness (a breakdown of market and social factors) against University Strengths in the Subject Area on a graph running from low to high. To illustrate, if high subject area attractiveness intersected with high university strength, the strategy would be "grow"; if both were medium, the strategy would be "consolidation"; and if both were low, "planned withdrawal and redeployment." It might be noted that while consolidation and withdrawal-redeployment occur in several combinations of events, growth is only advocated when strengths and attractiveness are both high. Individual universities and external financing bodies will define university strengths and future attractiveness of the subject area in different ways. A technological university may view its role differently from a long-established civic university. Thus additions and changes might be made to the list of factors for assessing university strengths in the subject area and subject area attractiveness. These might include service to the community, dependence on overseas students, or service to other subject areas.

The matrix could be developed at a number of levels: nationally by governmental and external financing bodies, regionally by groups of institutions, and individually by each institution. Presumably those governments that have regulated the size and type of overall intake by imposing formalized admission policies and criteria consider they have the resources and expertise to undertake the evaluations incorporated in the matrix and so justify increased dirigisme in terms of societal needs. Should collaborative approaches to rationalization be welcomed by governments and external financing bodies and be seen by institutions as an alternative to increased dirigisme? In the United Kingdom, the Committee of Vice-Chancellors and Principals (1980, p. 7) has recognized "the need to face more boldly the prospect of interinstitutional arrangements designed to promote some rationalization." In some countries institutions may well have to decide whether to compete or cooperate at the regional level.

As the Swedes have recognized in their institutional self-evaluation activity (Furumark, 1979), decentralized structures under conditions of financial stringency and possible contraction require institutions to critically study and evaluate themselves. Furthermore the absence in the United Kingdom of many of the features of the U.S. university system (for example, the close interface with the political decision-making process, the role of laymen in university government and the management of higher education, the strength of local community links, and the existence of well-recognized mechanisms for peer review) means that British universities have to find internal solutions to retrenchment—self-evaluation (Shattock, 1979). Similarly, peer review is hardly ever used in Sweden (Furumark, 1979). In other OECD countries there is a need to find internal solutions to retrenchment if institutional autonomy is to be preserved or at least not eroded further. The evaluation of subject areas by the university is a first stage in this evaluation, employing the criteria incorporated into the policy directional matrix or similar criteria. Comparing subject area attractiveness and university strengths provides a starting point from which managerial judgments can be made and for discussions on regional rationalization (see Figure 2). The decision makers in the institution need to systematically evaluate the trade-offs between strong and weak areas, and the administrators and academics should provide the framework and information base for this evaluation.

The growth, consolidation, and withdrawal and redeployment strategies are examples. Institutions may not wish to withdraw from all low-strength, low-attractiveness subject areas, but they should recognize the dangers and costs of not doing so. There is the obvious danger of increased government intervention if institutions are not prepared to put their own houses in order, or if they are not willing to cooperate regionally. A serious risk is that under conditions of stagnation or contraction the university will not be able to support existing developments and new developments in emerging areas which have high future attractiveness. Emerging areas can be supported out of incremental funds during periods of expansion, but not under conditions of stagnation or decline. Higgledy-piggledy expansion may have been acceptable in the past, but higgledy-piggledy stagnation or decline may not lead an institution to recognize the need to redeploy resources from low-strength, low attractiveness areas into emerging and existing growth areas. Thus, should institutions identify emerging growth areas as part of their study of the future needs of society, evaluate the skills and resources required to develop in these areas, and examine the extent to which the institution currently possesses or is able to acquire these skills and resources? To successfully enter these emerging growth areas it may be necessary to cross traditional departmental and school boundaries. It will also be recognized that existing subject areas which fall into the growth and consolidation categories should evaluate their teaching and research program to ensure that they remain relevant to the present and future needs of society. Self-evaluation and self-renewal should be encouraged in these areas.

The strategy that emerges from this evaluation of institutions' subject areas would distinguish between existing and emerging growth areas, consolidation areas, and withdrawal and redeployment areas. The agreed strategy would need to be translated into a detailed action

Figure 2. University Policy Directional Matrix

Size of Department;
Market Share;
Market Position;
Number of Applications;
Quality of Student Intake;
Graduate Employment;
Cost per FTE student;
Reputation;
Quality and age of staff;
Research record;
Research capability;
Image;
Publications record;
Resources: availability and mobility; and so on

UNIVERSITY STRENGTHS IN THE SUBJECT AREA

Market size;
Market growth rate;
Market diversity;
Competitive structure;
Cost structure;
Optimal Department size;

Demographic trends;
Scientific importance;
Technological trends;
Social/Political and Economic trends;
Environmental trends;
Government attitudes;
Employment prospects;
and so on

SUBJECT AREA ATTRACTIVENESS

	HIGH	MEDIUM	LOW
HIGH	Grow	Selective Growth or Consolidation	Consolidation
MED.	Selective Growth or Consolidation	Consolidation	Planned Withdrawal and Redeployment
LOW	Consolidation or Planned Redeployment	Planned Withdrawal and Redeployment	Planned Withdrawal and Redeployment

plan including key result areas. Measures to assess progress towards implementing the strategy, particularly in these key result areas, would flow from the plan. Thus, the Swedish National Board of Universities and Colleges considers: "Every activity evaluation project should, we think, result in an action-oriented, preferably long-range, plan for future activities, including indications of alternative ways to realize the desired changes" (Furumark, 1979, p. 11).

The strategic planning approach advocated here and elsewhere (Sizer, 1979a, 1979b, 1979c) should enable institutions to develop a set of alternative strategies and operating plans including strategies for long-term resource mobility. As changes in the external environment occur, the range of strategies can be narrowed down and the appropriate strategy and operating plan implemented. Under conditions of financial stringency and uncertainty, institutions may need to complement their long-term strategy for resource mobility with a short-term strategy for financial emergencies (Donaldson, 1969, 1970) and a medium-term strategy for financial mobility. The application of these concepts to colleges and universities has been examined by Dickmeyer (1980) in his contribution to the General Conference of the Institutional Management in Higher Education Programme. The existence of computer-based financial planning models will facilitate the preparation and updating of such strategies (Dickmeyer, Hopkins, and Massey, 1978).

Such models do not dismiss the uncertainty surrounding university planning but assist in understanding the nature of the uncertainty. They allow administrators to test the sensitivity of the plans to variations in key variables, to evaluate trade-offs and test tactical decisions, to revise plans quickly when variations in key variables do take place, and to identify key future performance indicators relating to the primary planning variables.

It is hoped the existence of parallel plans for short-term financial emergencies and medium-term financial mobility will ensure not only an appropriate speed of response to a rapidly changing exernal environment which is comptatible with the strategy for long-term resource mobility, but also increased flexibility in planning. It will help to ensure an appropriate balance is obtained between the pressure to increase cost efficiency in the short term and actions needed to be taken if the organization is to be effective in the long term.

Tests of Appropriateness

Clearly, a whole range of process, outcome, and progress performance indicators should be considered when establishing appropriate indicators for the research, teaching, and central service functions within an institution of higher education. Given that higher education abounds with joint inputs and multiple outputs and outcomes, and the ulitmate impact of many of the outcomes is long term and extremely difficult to measure, what tests should be applied to various possible indicators to determine whether they are appropriate for the purpose intended? Can the American Accounting Association (AAA) (1966) standards be applied to performance indicators in higher education? These are the four standards of relevance, verifiability, freedom from bias, and quantifiability. It should be recognized at the outset that trade-offs frequently have to be made between standards.

Relevance. Should relevance be the dominant test applied to any proposed or existing performance indicator? Is a relevant performance indicator one which bears upon the activity or is useful to those concerned with managing that activity? Who determines relevance? While the administrator should provide guidance, should it be the decision maker, either an individual responsible for the function to which an indicator relates or a policy committee, that oversees the function? Do we always recognize that a performance indicator may be relevant for the purpose for which it was developed, but not relevant when used for other purposes?

One of the major problems facing those who wish to produce (for internal planning, control, and resource-allocation purposes) financial performance indicators for the research and teaching functions in higher education is the unscrambling of joint costs of research and teaching functions and the central services that support them. It may be wise to recognize at the outset that it is not possible to unscramble the joint costs, and that any attempt to do so is riddled with assumptions that do not stand up to objective assessment and criticism. Most attempts to unscramble joint costs in institutions of higher education employ an absorption costing approach to produce full costs (Cossu, 1978).

Do university administrators who use such approaches to generate and supply financial indicators not only test their cost allocation procedures against the stated standards but also explain the assumptions underlying the indicators, and the uses that can and cannot be made of them, to those who receive and use the indicators? Do they always recognize:

1. There is no one way of apportioning joint costs to cost centers or absorbing joint costs into cost units. It is quite possible that two equally competent accountants would arrive at different unit costs from the same basic data.

2. In institutions of higher education a high proportion of the costs are fixed or period costs, therefore, the average costs are unsuitable for determining the incremental costs of extra or fewer students, or changes in course design; or the avoidable costs if a department is closed, or a course no longer offered.

3. Methods that allocate staff costs on such factors as the basis of diary analysis or timetable analysis do not answer the question: If the lecturer was not lecturing to this course, what would he be doing with his time? If the lecturer has to allocate his time to competing demands, is the cost of his meeting one demand the best alternative foregone, in other words, the opportunity cost, not the sunk cost of his salary will be paid regardless of how he allocates his time?

4. Nor do such systems consider societal costs of higher education, such as the opportunity costs and benefits to society of students attending institutions of higher education.

Verifiability. The American Accounting Association (1966, p. 10) defines verifiability as "that attribute of information which allows qualified individuals working independently of one another to develop essentially the same evidence, data, or research." In institutions of higher education is this an extremely important standard, when, for example, a performance indicator, such as staff-student ratio, is applied across a number of teaching departments, and subsequently forms an input into the resource allocation process? Is it unlikely that the absorption costing systems referred to above would meet this standard? Does the standard of verifiability aim at protecting the teaching department from arbitrary subjective judgments by those who use the data, and protect the user from similar judgments by those who generate the data? Given the democratic nature of institutions of higher education, is verifiability essential if harmonious relations are to exist between administrators and academics, and between heads of departments and units and resource allocating committees? If one accepts the continuing need for verifiability, one also recognizes the importance of reliable initial source data, data banks, and appropriate management information systems.

Freedom from Bias. Should the performance indicator be free from both statistical and personal bias? Statistical bias can result from inappropriate techniques of measurement, and personal bias from conscious manipulation of information for personal gain. This leads to the questions: Are the techniques of measurement appropriate? Can the performance indicator be manipulated by individuals to their advantage?

Quantifiability. How important is this standard to performance indicators in higher education? It may be necessary to trade off between quantifiability and relevance. Care must be taken not to give greater weight to quantifiable-less-relevant indicators than to non-quantifiable-but-relevant indicators. For example, number of research publications may be less relevant than the quality of research papers. The quality of lecturers' performances in classrooms may be more relevant than their average lecture hours. Östergren (1977, p. 8) has recognized that "activity evaluation is very liable to be dominated by those aspects of activities and results which are more amenable to quantitative description." He asks: "How can a proper balance be struck between qualitative and quantitative aspects?" Reports on French experience (Cuenin, 1978, and Fardeau, 1978) and studies conducted by the National Center for Higher Education Management Systems (Lawrence, Weathersby, and Patterson, 1970; Micek and Arney, 1974; Micek and Walhaus, 1973) and Chan (1978) in the U.S. confirm that this is a particularly relevant question when considering research performance indicators. Furthermore, as Romney (1978) has pointed out, if the external financing bodies continue to emphasize indicators of process, rather than progress, effectiveness, and efficiency when assessing institutions, administrators and faculty will begin, or continue, to function in accordance with incentive structures which are not consistent with an institution's goals and objectives. (See, for example, examinations by Gross, 1979, of formula budgeting and financing of public higher education in the U.S., and by Cuthbert and Birch, 1979, of the operations of the Advanced Further Education Pool in the United Kingdom.) Nevertheless, are relevant quantifiable performance indicators more likely to meet the tests of verifiability and freedom from bias than relevant qualitative and nonquantitative indicators?

Economic Feasibility. A fifth standard proposed by the American Accounting Association (1969) should also be applied to performance indicators in higher education. Having established appropriate performance indicators in the areas of teaching, research, and support services, accountants will recognize that an information system has to be developed for reporting physical measures of inputs and outputs and financial indicators (such as unit costs and agreed measures of progress toward institutional objectives developed by consensus-building techniques) to responsible management. However, will the cost of producing the performance indicator be outweighed by the benefit derived from its availability and use by decision makers? Economic feasibility is part of the trade-offs between relevance, freedom from bias, and verifiability. Fortunately, as the American Accounting Association (1969, p. 52) has pointed out, in institutions of higher education, as in other organizations, "the costs of gathering, storing, and presenting information are expected to decline in the future, so the standard of economic feasibility may be expected to encourage rather than deter requirements in information systems."

Balderston (1974, p. 103) has argued, "Universities will do well to install the best data systems they can afford and tolerate." Still, many would agree with Romney's view (1978, p. 36) that "throughout higher education the potential for information overload is overwhelming." While Somit (1979, p. 94) has suggested that "so long as universities enjoyed constantly increased funding, the fallacy that management decisions could be based almost entirely on information, if only we have enough, remained unchallenged. When that era ended, the inherent limitations of data, and of the systems which provided them, became all too apparent."

In theory the manager of a responsibility center, be it a service department, an academic department, or a research center, should be required to agree on objectives; to quantify targets; to evaluate and choose between alternatives; to plan and budget for the resources required; to organize, motivate, and direct those resources; and to compare actual performance against the plan and, when appropriate, take action on adverse deviations. The design and implementation of an information system to support this range of tasks is a demanding exercise even where objectives are clear cut, the output is well defined, and input-output relationships established. Baldridge and Tierney (1979) have recently examined the values of management information systems and management by objectives and have considered whether these techniques really help improve organizational processes. It has been emphasized that it is immensely more difficult in higher education "given the intangible and inherently immensurable nature of the values which pervade higher education and which, in the long run, determine our actions" (Somit, 1979, p. 94). Nevertheless, society and financing bodies are not prepared to exempt education managers from assessment in terms of their effectiveness and efficiency, and certainly they should be encouraged to assess their own performance. Therefore, despite Romney's and Somit's observations, provided the information system is economically feasible, should it concentrate on:

1. providing a base for planning and controlling resource utilzation;

2. monitoring the level of response to and outcomes of the institution's provision of learning opportunities, research facilities, and central services and expressing those responses in the form of nonfinancial and financial, quantitative performance indicators; and
3. monitoring agreed measures of progress toward institutional goals developed by consensus-building techniques, so as to provide a meaningful starting point from which qualitative managerial judgments can be made?

Institutional Acceptability. Porter (1978, p. 16) has proposed a further test be added to the five standards. He argues, "The measures of performance adopted may not themselves be the most reliable indicators of effectiveness or even efficiency, but they could be justified if they lead to improved performance or decision taking even though they themselves may not be thoroughly sound intellectually. What is vital is that the people using the indicators should accept them, and the basis on which they are devised, as relevant and fair." Is Porter recognizing the political realities of institutions of higher education? As Argyris (1970, p. 29) has pointed out: "New developments for rational decision making often produce intense resentment in men who ordinarily view themselves as realistic, flexible, definitely rational. Managers and executives who place a premium on rationality and work hard to subdue emotionality become resistant and combative in the back-alley ways of bureaucratic politics when such technologies are introduced."

Could "heads of departments and units" be substituted for "managers and executives" in Argyris's statement? Thus, is Romney (1978) right to argue, like Porter (1978), that consensus-building techniques, such as those described in his study, can facilitate the selection of appropriate goals and measures within institutions? Will such approaches result in economy of information by concentrating on the few highly appropriate goal areas for which a consensus exists, rather than trying to document progress in every goal area that has been accorded some degree of appropriateness?

Or should we recognize that such consensus building might be more easily achieved when resources are relatively abundant than when they are relatively scarce? A recent study undertaken by Hills and Mahoney (1978) of the nature of budget decision making in a university is relevant to this question. Their research indicated that relative abundance or scarcity of resources available for allocation is a significant influence in the budgeting process. They found that, while precedent was a significant influence in both situations, it was the predominant influence in the allocation of discretionary budget increments under conditions of abundant resources and a secondary influence under conditions of scarce resources. In this study the predominant influence during the period of scarce resources was externally based power represented by the existence of advisory boards, an influence not readily apparent during periods of abundant resources. Furthermore, a bureaucratic, or universalistic, criterion, relative workload, was influential in the period of abundant resources but had little influence during the period of scarce resources. Hills and Mahoney (p. 464) consider their results suggest that "subunit budgeting is a process designed, in part, to ameliorate conflict and to maintain apparent harmony. This is accomplished by the allocation of discretionary resources according to accepted standards (workload) and a proportionate, or fair share, criterion during periods of relative abundance of resources." This practice is consistent with Porter's standard of institutional acceptability.

Many of the resource allocation models described by Hussain (1976) employ an induced course-load matrix to generate resource entitlement by department. In an interesting critique of the planning system employed at the University of Aston in Birmingham, Houghton, Mackie, and Pietrowski (1979, p. 18) highlight the limitations of relative workload criteria as a basis for resource allocation under conditions of stagnation and financial stringency.

> The major characteristic of Aston's planning procedures, of which it has been justly proud in the past, is that it has been structured on a quantitative basis so that, in theory at least, academic departments forming the input can establish the output for themselves. A quantitative system, however, based largely on immediate past practice and the outcome of the previous year, can only function effectively in an expanding situation. . . . In a steady state or reducing situation, however, such as that now facing British universities, Aston's system allows little room for manoeuvre since there are in the plan no firmly established priorities as such: these have been expressed only in the broadest sense. . . . Thus the matching of academic planning desires with the financial resources available can only be achieved by cutting across the spectrum equally, or in planning jargon, "rateably reducing." The academic plan becomes a race in which everyone wins a prize but no one gets the gold medal.

Hills and Mahoney's research suggests that during periods of scarce resources, "It is the powerful subunits that emerge to claim their resources at the expense of other subunits. Further, it is the external ties that subunits have which they can use as this power base" (1978, p. 464). Under these conditions, is "cutting across the spectrum equally" acceptable to heads of powerful departments and do institutional acceptability and consensus building evaporate in Argyris's back-alley ways of bureaucratic politics? Nevertheless, it is suggested that these standards: relevance, verifiability, freedom from bias, quantifiability, economic feasibility, and institutional acceptablity, can usefully be applied to existing and proposed performance indicators in institutions of higher education.

Managers of Change

Debates in United Kingdom universities in response to a University Grants Committee planning exercise based on three possible levels of funding for a university for the quadrennium 1980-81 to 1983-84, modest growth, no change, and modest decline, have highlighted the need to employ consensus-building techniques and to avoid conflicts arising between the objectives, aspirations, and self-perceptions of departments, schools, and other faculty groups and the objectives of the institution. At the same time acceptance has to be obtained of the need for stronger central direction of the university than heads of departments and faculty have grown accustomed to. They have also highlighted the difficulties involved in consensus building, and the behavioral problems underlying institutional self-evaluation and self-renewal. Sadly, under today's conditions institutional acceptability and consensus building can easily evaporate in the "back-alleys."

It is in this context that the question is frequently posed: Can you manage change and achieve resource mobility during a period when institutions are likely to be more concerned with coping with the pressures of revised student numbers and lower provision per FTE? In other words, will the senior academics and administrators, the managers of change, in institutions of higher education be so concerned with today's problems that they will not give adequate consideration to tomorrow's (particularly when many of these managers of change may have retired before the 1990s)? Cyert (1977), a distinguished organizational theorist and president of Carnegie-Mellon, has emphasized that the trick of managing the contracting organization is to break the vicious circle which tends to lead to disintegration of the organization and that the management must develop counterforces which will allow the organization to maintain viability.

Furthermore, it is important to recognize that, although there are parallels with earlier periods of low growth in institutions, in many OECD countries significant changes have taken place in the status and attitudes of university lecturers. They feel there has been a significant lowering of their status in society and they have been badly treated by governments. They may face higher teaching loads at a time when their career opportunities have diminished significantly. Not only may they have less time for research, but, if there are few promotional prospects, they may well not feel motivated to undertake research of the type needed to cope with the dynamic changes in society anticipated (assuming research grants are available), and the unions that represent them may not accept, though they may recognize, the need for resource mobility and for lecturers' own retraining and redeployment. Thus, is the real danger of contraction that individuals who by nature desire excellence will, out of frustration, begin to settle for mediocrity (Cyert, 1978)?

Like Cyert, Sizer has argued elsewhere (1979a, 1979c) that there is a need to appoint high-quality managers of appropriate academic standing, when the opportunities arise, who can overcome institutional inertia. These managers of change should not only be able to plan and control efficiently the allocation of resources to see their institutions through the short-term financial pressures, but also be able to motivate people to recognize the need for long-term change and secure their participation in its planning and subsequent implementation. By gaining acceptance for phased withdrawal from some subject areas, they need to turn fixed costs into variable costs so as to release resources to finance new faculty and new initiatives in existing and emerging growth areas which are consistent with the institution's long-term objectives. They will recognize that innovations in response to new needs and new opportunities are frequently created through the initiative of individuals. If they are to break the vicious circle that leads to disintegration, they have to create an environment which motivates individuals and fosters rather than frustrates such initiatives.

To support these managers of change, governments will have to accept that it will be necessary to develop an appropriate incentive structure which will facilitate and not inhibit change; for example, more resources for staff retraining and development and generous early retirement schemes.

However, while Cyert (1977, p. 17) considers management "our major hope for the future" he also recognizes that "academics resist being managed by expert managers and seek to have an academic in the top management position. Only rarely will this approach lead to an excellent manager" (Cyert, 1978, p. 347). It may be for this reason that an anonymous registrar of a British university (1979, p. 9) has expressed the view that British universities find themselves without the apparatus for that efficient and effective deployment and management of scarce resources. He considers they are "hung up still on the medieval and almost superstitious fear of management within universities which leaves the resource allocation processes in many of them hardly able to stand comparison with an unsophisticated game of bingo." In Europe the Institutional Management in Higher Education Programme of OECD/CERI (Center for Educational Research and Innovation) has made a significant contribution to breaking down this fear of management.

The Hills and Mahoney study (1978) suggests that university budgeting in the U.S. may be characterized in a period of abundant resources by adherence to arbitrary rules and historical precedents and by the maintenance of stable relationships between subunits. It may be that during periods of scarcity of resources there will be greater competition for resources and questioning of arbitrary rules and historical precedents, but this may be resisted because of its potential disruptive effects upon subunit relationships. Do the decision makers within the institutions ask themselves whether their resource allocation formulas are compatible with their long-term objectives and strategies? Could their resource allocation processes be dysfunctional in this respect? Do the committees that make decisions about vacant posts take account of long-term strategies for resource mobility or simply concentrate on historical relative workload?

Overemphasis by external financing bodies on process performance indicators that measure short-term effectiveness and efficiency at the expense of progress measures might result in incentive situations which are not consistent with the institution's long-term goals and objectives, toward which the managers of change are striving. This is not to say that short-term cost efficiency is not important and process performance indicators are not relevant. It is a question of balancing short-term cost efficiency with long-term effectiveness. Certainly resource allocation processes compatible with the institution's strategy to achieve long-term goals and objectives may be inconsistent with the achievement of improved short-term cost efficiency.

Institutional Self-Evaluation

This chapter has examined the changing nature of performance assessment in the responsive university under conditions of changing needs of society, particularly during periods of contraction and under conditions of financial stringency. It has been argued that during such periods high-quality managers of change of appropriate academic standing should be motivating their institutions to strive to become effective in the long term through attempts

- to examine systematically the future environment in which it will be operating and to identify threats and opportunities
- to understand and communicate the implications of this future environment to the institution's constituencies
- to evaluate the institution's current subject area portfolio and critical resources
- to agree through consensus-building techniques the goals and objectives for the institution and its constituent parts, and the measures for monitoring progress toward achieving these goals and objectives.

Institutions should also be guided to develop (1) a set of alternative long-term strategies and operating plans including a strategy for long-term resource mobility; (2) a strategy for medium-term financial mobility and short-term emergencies; (3) resource allocation procedures consistent with the institution's long-term objectives; and (4) a short-term planning and control system based on measurable information and performance indicators, backed up by a nationally organized scheme for interinstitutional comparisons (Sizer, 1979a).

To achieve positive motivation, institutions of higher education are having to recognize that faculty and administrators at all levels should participate in all aspects of performance assessment, hence the growing interest in institutional self-evaluation and self-renewal. Drawing upon institutional experience in self-evaluation in Canada since 1975, Gingras and Girard (1979) have identified some preliminary conditions for preparing an institutional evaluation policy. There is considerable scope for further research.

A case has been made for the appointment of high-quality managers of change when opportunities arise who can build consensus within institutions and overcome the behavioral problems surrounding institutional self-evaluation. It will be recognized that there are at least three alternative models: the dominating, dictatorial vice-chancellor, president, or rector; the high-quality manager of conflict; and the *diri-*

giste government department or central body. Not only are these alternatives likely to be incompatible with the democratic nature of institutions, but they may create more behavioral problems than they solve and are unlikely to maintain institutional vitality and cohesiveness.

References

Allen, M. G. "Corporate Strategy and the New Environment." In *Strategic Leadership: The Challenge to Chairmen.* London: McKinsey, 1978.
American Accounting Association. *Statement of Basic Accounting Theory.* Evanston, Ill.: American Accounting Association, 1966.
American Accounting Association. "Report of the Committee on Managerial Decision Models." *The Accounting Review,* Supplement, 1969, *44,* 52.
Argyris, C. "Resistance to Rational Management Systems." *Innovation,* 1970, *10,* 29.
Balderston, F. E. *Managing Today's University.* San Francisco: Jossey-Bass, 1974.
Balderston, F. E. "Note on Professor Sizer's Paper." *International Journal of Institutional Management in Higher Education,* 1979, *3,* 1.
Baldridge, J. V., and Tierney, M. L. *New Approaches to Management.* San Francisco: Jossey-Bass, 1979.
Chan, J. L. "Organizational Consensus Regarding the Relative Importance of Research Output Indicators." *The Accounting Review,* 1978, *53* (2), 309-323.
Committee of Vice-Chancellors and Principals. *Memorandum to the United Kingdom.* Government's Select Committee on Education, Science, and the Arts, February 1980.
Cossu, C. "Costs: Tools for University Planning." *International Journal of Institutional Management in Higher Education,* September 1978, *2* (2), 207-220.
Cuenin, J. S. "Les Moyens Accordés à la Recherche Universitaire en France." Paper presented at the OECD/CERI-IMHE Program fifth special topic workshop, Paris, France, June 5-6, 1978.
Cuthbert, R. E., and Birch, D. W. "Resource Utilisation Performance Indicators in the Public Sector of Higher Education." Paper presented to annual conference of the Society for Research into Higher Education, Brighton Polytechnic, U.K., December 19-20, 1979.
Cyert, R. "Academic Progress and Stable Resources." Lecture given at National Center for Higher Education Management Systems, Denver, Colo., November 7, 1977.
Cyert, R. "The Management of Universities of Constant or Decreasing Size." *Public Administration Review,* July/August 1978.
Delany, V. J. "Budgetary Control and Monitoring Effectiveness." *Management Accounting,* October 1978, 388-391, 422.
Department of Education and Science. *Higher Education in the 1990s.* London: Department of Education and Science, 1978.
Department of Education and Science. *Future Trends in Higher Education.* London: Department of Education and Science, 1979.
Dickmeyer, N. "Balancing Risks and Resources: Financial Strategies for Colleges and Universities." Paper presented to the fifth general conference on the IMHE Program, OECD/CERI, Paris, France, September 8-10, 1980.
Dickmeyer, N., Hopkins, D. S. P., and Massey, W. F. "TRADES: A Model for Interactive Financial Planning." *Business Officer,* March 1978, pp. 22-27.
Donaldson, G. *Strategy for Financial Mobility.* Boston: Harvard University, 1969.
Donaldson, G. "Strategy for Financial Emergencies." *Harvard Business Review,* January 1970, pp. 67-79.

Doyle, P., and Lynch, J. E. "A Strategic Model for University Planning." *Journal of the Operational Research Society,* 1979, *30* (7), 603-609.

Fardeau, M. "Indicateurs de performance pour la fonction 'recherche' dans les établissements d'enseignement supérier." Paper presented to the OECD/CERI-IMHE Program fifth special topic workshop, Paris, France, June 5-6, 1978.

Furumark, A.-M. *Activity Evaluation in Higher Education, a Swedish Project.* Stockholm: Research and Development Division of the National Board of Universities and Colleges, 1979.

Gingras, P.-E., and Girard, M. "A Few Guidelines for an Institutional Evaluation Policy." *Institutional Analysis,* 1979, *11A,* Montreal, Le Centre d'animation de développement et de recherche en éducation (CADRE).

Gross, F. M. "Formula Budgeting and the Financing of Public Higher Education: Panacea or Nemesis for the 1980s?" *The AIR Professional File,* 1979, *3.*

Hecquet, I., and Jadot, J. *The Impact on University Management of Financing and Control Systems for Higher Education.* Summary Report of a Joint Project of IMHE Program (OECD/CERI) and L'Association des Universités Partiellement ou Entiêrement de Langue Francaise (AUPELF), 1978.

Hedley, B. "A Fundamental Approach to Strategy Development." *Long Range Planning,* December 1976, *9.*

Hedley, B. "Strategy and Business Portfolio." *Long Range Planning,* February 1977, *10.*

Hills, F. A., and Mahoney, T. A. "University Budgets and Organizational Decision Making." *Administrative Science Quarterly,* 1978, *23,* 454-465.

Houghton, K. N., Mackie, D., and Pietrowski, C. "The University of Aston in Birmingham." Case Study presented to the seventh professional seminar of the OECD/CERI-IMHE Program. Zurich, Swit.: September 1979.

Hussain, K. M. *Institutional Resource Allocation Models in Higher Education.* Paris: OECD Centre for Educational Research and Innovation, 1976.

Institutional Management in Higher Education (IMHE) Programme. "Survey on the State of the Art and Likely Future Trends." Report presented to the fifth general conference of the IMHE Program, OECD/CERI, Paris, France, September 8-10, 1980.

Jochimsen, R. "Managing Universities in the Eighties: Introductory Remarks." *International Journal of Institutional Management in Higher Education,* 1979, 3 (1), 5-20.

Lawrence, B., Weathersby, G., and Patterson, V. W. (Eds.). *Outputs of Higher Education: Their Identification, Measurement, and Evaluation.* Boulder, Colo.: Western Interstate Commission on Higher Education, 1970.

Micek, S. S., and Arney, W. R. *The Higher Education Outcome Measures Identification Study: A Descriptive Summary.* Denver, Colo.: National Center for Higher Education Management Systems, 1974.

Micek, S. S., and Walhaus, R. A. *An Introduction to the Identification and Uses of Higher Education Outcome Measures.* Denver, Colo.: National Center for Higher Education Management Systems, 1973.

Östergren, B. "Project Concerning Activity Analysis in Higher Education." *R & D for Higher Education,* 1977, *1,* 5-9.

Porter, D. "Developing Performance Indicators for the Teaching Function." Paper presented to the OECD/CERI-IMHE Program fifth special topic workshop, Paris, France, June 5-6, 1978.

Registrar of a Northern University. "British Universities: What Next?" *Times Higher Education Supplement,* December 28, 1979.

Robinson, S. J. Q., Hichens, R. E., and Wade, D. P. "The Directional Policy Matrix — Tool for Strategic Planning." *Long Range Planning,* 1978, *11,* 8-15.

Romney, L. C. *Measures of Institutional Goal Achievement.* Denver: National Center for Higher Education Management Systems, 1978.

Romney, L. C., Bogen, C., and Micek, S. S. "Assessing Institutional Performance: The Importance of Being Careful." *International Journal of Institutional Management in Higher Education,* 1979, *3* (1), 79-89.

Romney, L. C., Gray, R. C., and Weldon, H. K. *Departmental Productivity: A Conceptual Framework.* Denver: National Center for Higher Education Management Systems, 1978.

Shattock, M. L. "Retrenchment in U.S. Higher Education: Some Reflections on the Resilience of the U.S. and U.K. University Systems." *Education Policy Bulletin,* Institute for Post-Compulsory Education, University of Lancaster, 1979, *1,* 2.

Sizer, J. "Performance Assessment and the Management of Universities for the 1990s." Paper presented to Conference of University Administrators annual conference, Edinburgh, U.K., April 5-7, 1979a.

Sizer, J. "Assessing Institutiional Performance: An Overview." *International Journal of Institutional Management in Higher Education,* 1979b, *3* (1), 49-75.

Sizer, J. "Performance Indicators for Institutions of Higher Education Under Conditions of Financial Stringency, Contraction, and Changing Needs." Keynote address presented to annual conference of the Society for Research into Higher Education, Brighton Polytechnic, U.K., December 19-20, 1979c.

Sizer, J. "Performance Assessment in Institutions of Higher Education under Conditions of Financial Stringency, Contraction, and Changing Needs: A Management Accounting Perspective." Paper presented to third annual congress of the European Accounting Association, Amsterdam Free University, Neth., March 24-26, 1980a.

Sizer, J. "Institutional Performance Assessment Under Conditions of Changing Needs." Expository paper presented to fifth general conference of the IMHE Program, OECD/CERI, Paris, France, September 8-10, 1980b.

Somit, A. "Management Information Systems: Neither Paradise Lost nor Paradise Gained." *International Journal of Institutional Management in Higher Education,* 1979, *3* (1), 91-94.

Sorenson, J. R., and Grove, H. D. "Cost-Outcome and Cost-Effectiveness Analysis: Emerging Nonprofit Performance Evaluation Techniques." *The Accounting Review,* 1977, *52* (3), 658-675.

John Sizer is senior pro-vice-chancellor and professor of financial management at the University of Technology, Loughborough, U.K. He is chairman of the directing group of the Institutional Management in Higher Education Programme of OECD and acts as senior adviser on institutional performance assessment to the organization. His publications include An Insight into Management Accounting *(Penguin Books, 1979),* Case Studies in Management Accounting *(Penguin Books, 1979), and* Perspectives in Management Accounting *(William Heinemann Ltd., 1980).*

The needs for careful research and study in institutional evaluation are manifold, but it is as important that educators monitor and guide the political and developmental aspects of this area. There will be pressure to adopt overly simple solutions to complex and sensitive problems. The best defense is a good offense — better ideas and approaches.

Some Concluding Remarks

Richard I. Miller

There is little doubt that institutional evaluation will be a much more predominant part of the postsecondary education scene in the 1980s than it was in the 1970s. This means we have ample opportunity to make a decisive impact if we give sufficient research attention, exercise political savvy, and oppose with rigorous vigor those who propose simplistic and misleading solutions to complex problems. It would be dangerous to throw up our hands and propose to study, without action. Sometimes the demands for decisions will not wait very long.

There are several potential trouble spots that need careful watching. Some studies reach misleading conclusions. A case in point are the "financial health" indexes (Lupton, Augenblick, and Heyison, 1976). A major criticism of the study is related to mistaken identity — that it is a mistake to equate financial health with academic excellence. Members of governing boards often are successful businessmen who are accustomed to equating a successful bottom line with a successful business. But a well-managed and efficient college may not be a place where excellent teaching and research take place. A financially healthy institution may have a dynamic learning environment or it may be dullsville. We must appraise teaching and program excellence primarily by criteria other than fiscal health.

Another potential trouble spot relates to state funding formulas. They were primarily developed during the 1960s and 1970s to provide an equitable way of distributing state funds, but even in halcyon days of expansion the public colleges and universities thought they needed more resources than they were allotted. These formulas, however, are obsolete in an era when many public institutions are holding their own or declining. While student revenues may remain about stationary, the inflationary costs for salaries, services, and resources considerably overshadow the modest gains in state revenues. Add the greater competition for public monies from the other sectors and the fiscal support picture for the 1980s is one of diminished net resources available to colleges and universities.

The importance of careful planning for institutional evaluation has been developed throughout this volume. The guidelines which follow were considered basic to the process.

- Vigorous and sensitive administrative leadership is crucial to effective institutional appraisal
- An overall evaluation plan should be developed and communicated
- The process of institutional appraisal is as important as the product
- Institutional evaluators should use objective data where available and appropriate but make no apologies for using subjective data (or, it is better to be generally right than precisely wrong)
- Institutional evaluation should be pragmatic, with plans for moving reports to action, and
- A plan for evaluating the evaluation should be included (Miller, 1979, pp. 283-288).

Finally, institutional evaluation should be a means and not an end. Self-study efforts that are undertaken for accreditation purposes make a fundamental error if they view the purposes of accreditation to be the end when, in fact, the effort should be the means that allows the institution to move toward meeting some obvious needs in some well-planned direction Accrediting associations are encouraging institutions to use the accreditation self-study for other purposes. The challenge is upon institutions to creatively design their evaluations to serve multiple ends.

References

Lupton, A. H. Augenolick, J., and Heyison, J. "The Financial State of Higher Education." *Change*, 1976, *8*, 20-38.

Miller, R. I. *The Assessment of College Performance: A Handbook of Techniques and Measures for Institutional Self-Evaluation.* San Francisco: Jossey-Bass, 1979.

Richard I. Miller is visiting fellow in the Department of Education at Cornell University. He is the author of three Jossey-Bass books on evaluation, the most recent being The Assessment of College Performance *(1979).*

Index

A

Academic growth, and educational quality, 52–53
Accreditation: action resulting from, 29; and college impact, 49–52; and educational program, 46, 54–55; and educational quality, 45–59; and faculty, 46, 55; and financial resources, 46, 55; as inferential approach, 47; and institutional assessment, 16–17, 22–23; and institutional goals, 46, 54; and library/learning center, 46, 47, 55–56; standards of, related to quality, 54–56; validation of standards for, 49–51; weaknesses of, 56–58
Advanced Further Education Pool, 77
Allen, M. G., 70, 85
American Accounting Association, 75, 76, 77, 78, 85
American Council on Education, 2, 4, 7
American Society for Engineering Education, 40
Andersen, C. J., 2, 4, 7, 14
Appropriateness, tests of, 74–81
Argyris, C., 79, 81, 85
Arney, W. R., 77, 86
Arns, R. G., 19, 21, 22, 25
Assessment. *See* Institutional assessment; Self-assessment
Astin, A. W., 9, 12, 13, 50, 52, 53, 55, 56, 58
Aston, University of, planning system at, 80
Augenblick, J., 89, 90

B

Baird, L. L., 8, 14
Balderston, F. E., 66, 78, 85
Baldridge, J. V., 78, 85
Bias, freedom from, appropriateness of, 76
Birch, D. W., 77, 85
Blackwell, G. W., 31, 37, 39, 42
Bogen, C., 62, 87
Boston Consulting Group, 69–70
Bradford, University of, Management Center at, 69
Brooklyn College, self-assessment at, 38

C

California, reputational ratings in, 5, 6
Campagna, D., 53, 58
Campbell, J. P., 20, 22, 25
Canada, self-evaluation in, 84
Cartter, A. M., 2, 4, 7, 13, 14, 53, 56, 58
Casey, R. J., 47, 58
Center for Educational Research and Innovation, 83
Centra, J. A., 52–53, 55, 56, 59
Chan, J. L., 77, 85
Change: and institutional assessment, 21, 24–25; managers of, 81–83
Chickering, A. W., 53, 54, 58
Clark, B. R., 16, 25
Clark, M. J., 8, 14
Clarkson College of Technology, self-assessment at, 32, 38, 40
Coleman, J. S., 54, 58
Commission on Higher Education of the Middle States Association of Colleges and Schools, 46–47, 54, 58
Commission on Institutions of Higher Education — New England Association of Schools and Colleges, 47, 58
Committee of Vice-Chancellors and Principals, 68, 71, 85
Cooperative Institutional Research Program, 6
Corning Community College, self-assessment at, 33, 38, 40, 42
Cossu, C., 75, 85
Cuenin, J. S., 77, 85
Cuthbert, R. E., 77, 85
Cyert, R., 81, 82, 83, 85

D

Dearing, B., 28, 31, 34, 42
Delany, V. J., 66, 85
Department of Education and Science, 62, 85

Dickmeyer, N., 74, 85
Donaldson, G., 74, 85
Doyle, P., 69-70, 86

E

Economic feasibility, appropriateness of, 77-79
Educational program: and accreditation, 46, 54-55; and reputational ratings, 12
Educational Testing Service, 53, 58
Exxon Education Foundation, 1*n*

F

Faculty: and accreditation, 46, 55; and reputational ratings, 3, 7; and self-assessment, 32; status of, 82
Fardeau, M., 77, 86
Feldman, K. A., 50, 51, 58
Financial health indexes, 89
Financial resources, and accreditation, 46, 55
France, institutional assessment in, 77
Fund for the Improvement of Post-Secondary Education (FIPSE), viii, 30, 31
Furumark, A.-M., 71, 74, 86

G

General Electric, 70
Germany, Federal Republic of, institutional assessment in, 61
Gingras, P.-E., 84, 86
Girard, M., 84, 86
Goals, institutional, and accreditation, 46, 54
Goodrich, H. B., 53, 58
Gourman, J., 5, 6, 14
Graduate education, reputational ratings of, 2-4
Graduate Record Examination Aptitude Test, 52, 55
Graduate Record Examination Area Tests, 52, 53, 55
Grambsch, P. V., 54, 58
Gray, R. C., 62, 87
Green, K. C., ix, 4, 5, 14
Gross, E., 54, 58
Gross, F. M., 77, 86
Grove, H. D., 63, 87

H

Haggerty, M. E., vii, ix
Harris, J. W., 47, 58
Hartnett, R. T., 8, 14, 20, 25
Hecquet, I., 68, 86
Hedley, B., 69, 86
Heyison, J., 89, 90
Hichens, R. E., 70, 86
Higher Education General Information Survey, 6
Higher Education Research Institute, 1-14
Hills, F. A., 79-80, 81, 83, 86
Hofstra University, self-assessment at, 37, 40
Holland, J. L., 53, 58
Hopkins, D. S. P., 74, 85
Houghton, K. N., 80, 86
Hoylman, F. M., 23, 26
Hughes, R. M., 2, 3, 4, 14
Hussain, K. M., 80, 86

I

Illinois, reputational ratings in, 5
Institutional acceptability, appropriateness of, 79-81
Institutional assessment: accreditation related to, 45-59; appropriateness in, tests of, 74-81; and autonomy, 71-73; and change, 21, 24-25, 81-83; current status of, 16-19; cyclical agenda for, 22-23; design of process for, 23-24; European perspective on, 61-87; future needs in, 66-68; and goal achievement, 20; guidelines for, 90; history of, vii; as internal activity, 15-26; issues in, 89-90; and leadership, 21; and markets, 69-71; and motivation of, 20; partial performance indicators for, 62-66; and policy directional matrices, 70-71; portfolio analysis for, 68-74; by reputational ratings, 1-14; by self-assessment, 27-43, 84-85; suggestions for, 21-25; theory of, 19-21
Institutional Management in Higher Education (IMHE) Programme, 62-63, 67-68, 74, 83, 86
Institutions: assessment within, 18-19; impact of, 49-52
Isocrates, vii

J

Jacob, P. E., 53, 55, 58
Jadot, J., 68, 86
Jencks, C., 54, 58
Jesse, R. H., vii
Jochimsen, R., 61, 67, 86
John Jay College of Criminal Justice, self-assessment at, 34, 37
Johnson, R. R., 8, 14

K

Kearney, R. C., 3, 14
Kells, H. R., vii-viii, 15-26, 30, 42
Keniston, H., 2, 4, 14
Kirkwood, R., 17, 21, 25
Knapp, R. H., 53, 58

L

Lawrence, B., 77, 86
Lawrence, J. K., vii, ix, 1-14
Learned, W. S., 51-52, 55, 58
Lehman, I. J., 53, 55, 58
Library/learning center, and accreditation, 46, 47, 55-56
Lindquist, J., 21, 24, 26
Linn, R. L., 52-53, 55, 56, 59
Lupton, A. H., 89, 90
Lynch, J. E., 69-70, 86

M

McDowell, J., 53, 58
Mackie, D., 80, 86
Magoun, H. W., 3, 14
Mahoney, T. A., 79-80, 81, 83, 86
Marist College, self-assessment at, 40
Marymount Manhattan College, self-assessment at, 34, 37
Massey, W. F., 74, 85
Micek, S. S., 62, 77, 86, 87
Middle States Association of Colleges and Schools, 46-47, 54, 58
Miller, R. I., vii-ix, 89-91
Morgan, D. R., 3, 14

N

National Board of Universities and Colleges, 74
National Center for Higher Education Management Systems, 77
National Merit Scholarship Qualifying Test, 52
National Research Council, 11, 14
New England Assocation of Schools and Colleges, 47, 58
New York: reputational ratings in, 5, 6; self-assessment in, 27-43
New York Bureau of College Evaluation, 29, 30, 32
New York City Community College, self-assessment at, 35
New York State Education Department, 29
New York State Task Force on Self-Assessment, 30, 31, 35
Newcomb, T. M., 50, 51, 58
Nichols, R. C., 52, 55, 56, 59
North Carolina, reputational ratings in, 5
North Central Association of Colleges and Schools—Commission on Institutions of Higher Education, vii, 47, 59
Northwest Association of Schools and Colleges—Commission on Colleges, 46, 48, 59

O

Orlans, H., 32, 34, 35, 41, 42
Östergren, B., 77, 86

P

Palola, E. G., 42
Parrish, R., 17, 25
Patterson, V. W., 77, 86
Pennsylvania, college impact in, 51-52, 55
Pennsylvania, University of, rating of graduate departments at, 2, 4
Peterson, M. W., 36, 41, 43
Pietrowski, C., 80, 86
Pigge, F. L., 22, 26
Poland, W., 19, 21, 22, 25
Polytechnic Institute of New York, self-assessment at, 40
Porter, D., 79, 80, 86

Q

Quality, educational: and accreditation, 45-59; correlates of, 51-54; defining, 48-49; and reputational ratings, 12-13; standards related to, 54-56
Quantifiability, appropriateness of, 77

R

Regens, J. L., 3, 14
Regents of New York, 29, 30
Relevance, appropriateness of, 75-76
Reputational ratings: analysis of, 1-14; components of, 2; and education, 12; and faculty eminence, 3, 7; findings of, 9-10; of graduate departments, 2-4; issues in, 1-2, 10-13; pilot study of, 4-10; purposes of, 3-4; and quality, 12-13; study design for, 5-9; of top domain, 11-12
Robinson, S. J. Q., 70, 86
Rock, D. A., 52-53, 55, 56, 59
Romney, L. C., 62, 63, 66, 77, 78, 79, 86-87
Roose, K. D., 2, 4, 7, 14

S

Scholastic Aptitude Test, 53
Self-assessment: analysis of, 27-43; budgeting for, 32-33; checklist of issues in, 33-34; data important in, 38; definition of, 30-31; external consultants for, 40; and faculty, 32; history of, 28-30; and inventory of past evaluations, 38-39; involvement in, 34-35; and leadership, 32; local resources for, 39-40; methods for, 38-41; obstacles to, 28, 31-36; planning for results of, 40-41; principles of, 36-38; priorities of, 37; purposes of 27-28; responsibility for, 33; results of, 41-42; self-adjustment of, 38
Shattock, M. L., 71, 87
Shell Group, 70
Sherwood, J. J., 23, 26
Sizer, J., viii-ix, 61-87
Solmon, L. C., vii, 1-14
Somit, A., 78, 87
Sorenson, J. R., 63, 87
Southern Association of Colleges and Schools, 46, 47, 59
State agencies, and institutional assessment, 17-18
State funding formulas, 90
State University of New York Agricultural and Technical College at Delhi, self-assessment at, 36, 37
State University of New York at Binghamton, self-assessment at, 32, 33, 37
State University of New York College at Gennesee, self-assessment at, 39
State University of New York College at Oswego, self-assessment at, 35
State University of New York College at Plattsburgh, self-assessment at, 33, 40
Sweden, institutional assessment in, 71, 74

T

Thistlethwaite, D. L., 53, 59
Tierney, M. L., 78, 85
Tritschler, D., viii, 27-43
Troutt, W. E., viii, 45-59

U

Undergraduate education, reputational ratings of, 1-14
United Kindgom, institutional assessment in, 62, 67, 68, 69, 71, 77, 80, 81, 83
University Grants Committee, 81

V

Verifiability, appropriateness of, 76
Veterans' Readjustment Act of 1952, 29

W

Wade, D. P., 70, 86
Wagner College, self-assessment at, 34
Walhaus, R. A., 77, 86
Warren, J. R., 16, 17, 26
Weathersby, G., 77, 86
Weldon, H. K., 62, 87
Western Association of Schools and Colleges, 47, 59
Wood, B. D., 51-52, 55, 58

Y

Youn, T. I. K., 16, 25
Young, K., 26

Z

Zook, G. F., vii, ix